Stations From The Air

JD Smith & Webbaviation.co.uk

SBP
Publishing

Contents

Introduction

For the first time, Stations From The Air brings together a full-colour collection of aerial photographs of some of the UK's largest railway stations and associated rail infrastructure, including restored heritage lines, famous rail bridges, and former stations.

All of the images in this book have been taken from the library of Webb Aviation. Run by Jonathan CK Webb, the UK's leading aerial photographer, the Webb Aviation library is the largest free online aerial photography gallery in the world with an average of over 4.5 million hits per month, and can be viewed at www.webbaviation.co.uk. Based at City Airport Manchester, Jonathan's expertise and years of experience in aerial photography make him the ideal person to photograph one of the most important features of the urban British landscape.

As well as the images, the book includes a fascinating history of each station, along with facts and figures. These figures include passenger numbers as recorded by the Office of Rail Regulation, with details from the last available five years shown. These figures include the combined number of passengers arriving and departing from each station, but not those making interchanges. The ranking for each station, out of a total of 2,518 stations, is also given. As can be seen in the figures, many smaller towns in the south of England have much higher numbers of passengers than larger towns and cities in the rest of the UK. This is due to the "London Effect" of millions of commuters regularly travelling into the capital city. Because of this, a town's ranking may be surprisingly low compared to what you would expect it to be.

Locomotives at Haworth

The Railways

For many people, a railway station is nothing more than the start or finish of a journey from point A to point B. It is likely that most people who use their local station will not even give a single thought as to its history or origins, or even its importance to their towns.

In our largest towns the railways cover a vast area that is not always too evident from street level. It is only from the air that we can truly see and appreciate the scale of the railways and our stations. The aerial images in this book not only show us the structures that are still standing, but also allow us to see the footprints of the past, with remnants of lost buildings, railway yards and even whole stations still visible where they would not be from the ground.

The railway age was a product of the Industrial Revolution and is a supreme example of British engineering and ingenuity. Human or animal powered railways had existed for centuries before the Industrial Revolution, but it wasn't until the invention of the steam engine in 1712 by Thomas Newcomen that the seeds for powered locomotion were sown. Newcomen's engine was the first workable design used to pump water out of mines. His engine was stationary, but as the technology developed during the 18th century, particularly with the improvements introduced by James Watt, the practicality of a moveable engine got closer.

The first successful demonstration of a steam locomotion engine took place on December 24th 1801. Called the "Puffing Devil", it was designed by Richard Trevithick, and was the precursor to the first proper railway journey. This took place on February 21st 1804, when one of Trevithick's engines carried 70 men and five wagons laden with iron ore for a distance of nearly ten miles on the Penydarren Tramway, near Merthyr Tydfil.

Huddersfield Station's magnificent façade

The platforms at Leeds City Station

In 1812 the world's first rack & pinion steam railway was to open in Middleton, Leeds, transporting coal from nearby collieries to the canals. This was followed in 1825 by the creation of the Stockton & Darlington Railway, the world's first passenger railway, and George Stephenson's famous "Locomotion No 1" engine. The world's first inter-city railway between Liverpool & Manchester was already being developed at this time, being founded on May 24th 1823. After its opening in 1830 the development of the railways snowballed.

Railway companies sprang up all over Great Britain, and in turn Britain exported them to the world. Many of these companies were small affairs between local towns, as businessmen and entrepreneurs saw the chance to get rich via haulage of goods and passengers. There was fierce, often ruthless, competition between rival companies, and it wasn't uncommon for towns to have several stations owned by different companies, often right next to each other. The companies were usually named after the routes on which their lines would travel, but gradually larger firms began to take a hold in the market, creating some of the most iconic names in British railway history, such as the London & North Western (LNWR) or the Great Western Railway (GWR). These bigger firms not only had the clout to finance new lines,

they also started to build their own locomotives, carriages and wagons, and also to take over the smaller companies.

The sights, sounds and smells of the steam locomotive have thrilled many a young boy over the years, but the pre-eminence of steam began to be threatened by the turn of the 20th century. The emergence of electrical locomotives in the late 19th century did not immediatel signal the end of steam power, as two World Wars saw the railway system come into its prime. The railway's played a vital part in the mobilisation of troops and supplies in both conflicts, but especially in the Second World War and the D-Day landings.

By this time the "Big Four" railway companies of the GWR, the LNWR, the London, Midland & Scottish (LMS) and the Southern Railway (SR) had been set up under the "1921 Grouping Act", which came into operation in 1923. The railways were taken under national control during WWI, and remained so until this act was enforced. It was designed to streamline the workings of the railway system and to stem financial losses. At its height there had been over 120 railway companies throughout the country, but not all of them had the resources to provide the services that they offered. Although a few other companies remained outside of this act, the "Big Four" was the first step towards nationalisation in 1948, with the formation of British Rail.

With the introduction of diesel powered locomotives in the 1950s, the days of steam were finally numbered. The last steam-powered passenger service ran on main line tracks in 1968, signalling the end of an era. It was all change for the railways in the 1960s, and not necessarily for the better. The infamous "Beeching Axe", which refers to the cutback of the national rail system by "The Reshaping of British Railways" report by Dr Richard Beeching in March 1963, would see the railways changed almost irrevocably. Over 3,000 stations were closed as a consequence of the report, along with over 7,000 miles of track, as the motor car became King. British Rail itself was not to last, and was privatised in the 1990s.

The railways are here to stay though, and in recent years passenger numbers have risen dramatically across the board, as people look to escape the growing congestion of the roads or find a cheaper form of transport. New stations are being built and old ones redeveloped, and there have even been plans to reopen some of the old lines where the routes allow. After over 200 years of history since the first railway journey, the future still looks bright for rail travel and our railway stations.

Altrincham

Opened: 03/04/1881

Platforms: 4
(2 National Rail, 2 Metrolink)

Passengers* (Rank):
2008/9: 260,882 (1100)
2007/8: 282,958 (989)
2006/7: 223,338 (1055)
2005/6: 210,021 (1017)
2004/5: 193,755 (1025)
*National Rail Only

The Cheshire market town of Altrincham is served by a dual-purpose station, being open for National Rail services as well as the Manchester Metrolink tram. The station was originally constructed by the Manchester, South Junction and Altrincham Railway and was named "Altrincham & Bowden", with the line running from Manchester London Road (Now Manchester Piccadilly) to its terminus here at Altrincham, a distance of eight and a half miles. The station was built to replace a previous station opened in July 1849. The entire route was closed at the end of 1991 and converted to Metrolink use; the first new tram system in the UK for decades. The lines reopened on June 15th 1992. This was part of the first phase of the tram system, and made up the southern arm of the system, officially known as the "Altrincham Line".

A Metrolink tram bound for Manchester can be seen in the photograph in the middle right. The trams run from platforms 1 and 2 on the western side. These are now bay platforms, as can be seen from the track reaching a dead-end on the left of the image. National Rail services still operate at the station and run from platforms 3 and 4 to Manchester Piccadilly via Stockport and to Chester in the opposite direction. The station is now usually referred to as "Altrincham Interchange" due to the construction of a new adjoining bus station in 1976. Of note is the freestanding station clock tower on a small island just by the main road (Stamford New Road). The tower was part of the original 1881 buildings and is now a Grade II listed structure.

Ashford International

Opened: 01/12/1842

Platforms: 6

Passengers (Ranking):
2008/9: 2,758,886 (131)
2007/8: 2,819,499 (120)
2006/7: 2,606,065 (122)
2005/6: 2,408,539 (104)
2004/5: 2,286,350 (108)

The first railway built in the town of Ashford was constructed by the South Eastern Railway company in 1842. The station survived relatively untouched until it was rebuilt between 1961 and 1963, a time that saw the electrification of the lines. Around this time, a new maintenance facility named Chart Leacon (left) was also constructed about a mile to the west of the station. The depot was built to services the newly introduced fleet of EMU's that would use the electrified lines. The main heavy repair depot, with its four pitched roofs, is over 610 feet long and around 220 feet wide. Ashford station was completely rebuilt again in the 1990s to enable it to handle Eurostar services. The new station featured a new island platform to the north (platforms 5 and 6), and an adjoining entrance hall, which can be seen protruding into the car park. This part of the complex is now often referred to simply as "Ashford Station" as it deals with domestic services. A new, much larger International station and concourse was built at the south of the station in 1996, opening on September 6th. International trains use platforms 3 and 4, the middle of the three island platforms, whilst domestic services use the remaining four platforms.

Bath Spa

Opened: 31/08/1840

Platforms: 2

Passengers (Ranking):
2008/9: 4,757,904 (67)
2007/8: 4,478,305 (67)
2006/7: 4,244,776 (72)
2005/6: 3,905,144 (62)
2004/5: 3,726,900 (65)

Now the main station in the historic city of Bath, Bath Spa occupies a site adjacent to the River Avon on the southeastern fringes of the city centre. The station itself is of historic importance as it was part of Isambard Kingdom Brunel's Great Western Railway that linked London with Bristol. Like almost all of the buildings in Bath, the station buildings are constructed of the same honey-coloured limestone that has come to represent the city and its elegant streets. The main station building, which is situated on the north side of the site, facing the city centre, is Grade II* listed. Despite only having two platforms, the station is now handling close to 5 million passengers per year, with the popularity of the city as a commuter base and a tourist destination contributing to these impressive figures. Of note is the unusually large distance between the eastbound and westbound tracks, which can be clearly seen in the centre of the image between the platforms. This is a legacy of the GWR broad gauge track, which at 7 feet and ¼ of an inch was much wider than the standard gauge of 4 feet 8 ½ inches now used throughout the UK. The GWR originally held-out in changing to standard gauge, but its lines were finally converted in 1892. The station underwent a large overhaul following the upgrade to the tracks in 1897. This resulted in the original overall roof, which had covered both the platforms and the tracks, being removed and replaced with the existing awnings. The old platforms, which were considerably smaller, about the length of the existing main building, were also extended in the rebuild. The land now occupied by the bus station (centre left) was the site of the old goods warehouse that was raised up on supporting pillars to reach the level of the tracks.

Bath Green Park (disused)

Opened: 07/05/1870

Closed: 07/03/1966

Platforms: 2

Constructed by the Midland Railway, Green Park Station was the terminus of the Mangotsfield and Bath Branch Line, with the first passenger service opening for business on August 4th 1869. At this time the station was not complete, and so the line had to stop at a temporary station a few hundred yards to the west of the Green Park site, on the opposite bank of the Avon. For much of its life the station was actually known as Queen Square Station, and only became Green Park as late as 1951. Despite its size, the station only had two platforms, with the space in-between used as sidings. Along with the Midland, the station was used by the Somerset & Dorset Railway, who obtained powers to use the station and the last half mile of track as part of their own line from Bournemouth. S&DR services began on July 20th 1874 when the line was completed, but the cost nearly forced the

company into bankruptcy, and so they leased it out to the Midland and the London & South Western a year later on a 999 year deal. The lands that had been home to the temporary terminus would go on to be the site of the main goods yard, with sheds for both the Midland and the S&DR. Sadly, Green Park Station was not to last, and would fall under the axe of the Beeching cull. It closed to passenger services in 1966. The impressive façade, again built in Bath-stone, has ensured the station has been granted listed status as a Grade II building. The remaining tracks leading into the station were ripped up in the early 1980s to allow a supermarket development, which can be seen in the top right. The station is now used for events and as a weekend market place.

Birmingham New Street

Opened: 01/06/1854

Platforms: 13

Passengers (Ranking):
2008/9: 25,191,945 (9)
2007/8: 17,007,185 (16)
2006/7: 14,525,873 (14)
2005/6: 17,303,169 (12)
2004/5: 16,243,912 (12)

New Street Station is one of the largest and busiest railway stations in Great Britain, being located at the centre of the country in one of its largest cities. It is also one of the stations that divides opinions most. The Station no longer bears any resemblance to its original construction and presently resembles a giant concrete behemoth. It officially opened in 1854, but construction had started in 1846 with the first rail services beginning in 1851. When it opened, the station had a classic barrelled roof which was 840ft long with a 212-foot span. Built by the London and North Western Railway, it was the largest roof of its kind in the world. Due to increased demand in services a second station was built on the western side of the site by the Midland Railway in 1885. Opening in February, this new addition had an equally impressive double-arched roof, with spans of 58 feet by 620 feet, and 67 ½ feet by 600 feet. The two stations were split by a cab road in the middle, Queen's Drive, the remnants of which can be seen over the platforms at the bottom of the image on the left hand page. Today, hardly any of these two stations remain. The station was bombed during World War II which led to the

removal of the LNWR roof between 1948 and 1952. This in turn led to new awnings being constructed over the platforms which greatly altered the look of the station, but that was nothing compared with what was to follow. New Street Station was completely redesigned during the 1960s into the structure that we see today. Officially opened in 1967, the new station has been submerged under a giant shopping complex, office block and car park. Where once the internal area was bright and spacious, it is now dark, damp and devoid of character, leading the station to be regularly voted as one of the worst in the country. All of this is set to change, however, following the start of a £600m redevelopment plan. Work started in April 2010 on creating a new station fit for the 21st century. New Street will gain a huge new concourse with improved passenger and retail facilities inside a giant atrium, along with a new façade made from reflective steel. The station currently handles almost twice as many passengers as it was designed to do following the last rebuild, but the capacity of the station is expected to double once the works are completed in 2015.

Birmingham Snow Hill

Opened: 01/10/1852

Platforms: 4
(3 National Rail, 1 Midlands Metro)

Passengers* (Ranking):
2008/9: 4,030,223 (78)
2007/8: 2,407,283 (162)
2006/7: 1,938,950 (193)
2005/6:   293,788 (819)
2004/5:   295,937 (795)
*National Rail Only

Snow Hill has enjoyed a turbulent history of closure and rebirth throughout its 150 years. Originally a grand GWR station on the Wolverhampton line, it was opened as "Birmingham Station" and was known as "Great Charles Street" and "Livery Street" before the name "Snow Hill" was adopted in February 1858. It featured an impressive booking hall and a beautiful Great Western Hotel at the front of the station. The act to build the station had initially been given to the Birmingham & Oxford Junction Railway, but the GWR absorbed the company in August 1848. The station was rebuilt between 1906 and 1912, resulting in the creation of 4 through platforms and 4 bay platforms. However, due to the length of the through platforms (around 1197 feet) they were each split into two platforms with numbers at

either end, to give the station an overall total of 12. After the Beeching report the station closed in March 1972, following on from the demolition of the hotel, amid much protest, in 1969. The station itself was demolished in 1977, only to be rebuilt a decade later with a multi-storey car park above. The current station has 4 platforms, with the eastern most platform (here seen at the bottom of the image) used as the terminus for the Midland Metro tram service from Wolverhampton, which opened in 1999. In the bottom right of the image, the remains of the older platforms can be seen either side of the current platforms, helping to show the scale of the original tracks.

urzon Street's brief existence as a passenger
tation came to an end with the construction
f Birmingham New Street by the London &
orth Western Railway. The station was built
y the London & Birmingham Railway and the
rand Junction Railway, with both companies
onstructing terminuses here within a year of
ach other in 1838 and 1839. However, when
he two companies merged to form the LNWR
1846 they started work on New Street at a
nore favourable city centre location, which
vould ultimately prove to be the death knell
or Curzon Street. Most passenger services
ad stopped by 1854, and they finished
ompletely by 1893. The station then
urvived until 1966 as a goods yard, the
ootprint of which we can see today.

(Continued, below right)

Opened: 24/06/1838

Closed to Passengers:
22/05/1893

Closed completely: 1966

Birmingham
Curzon Street (Site of)

The only surviving part of the original Curzon Street Station
is the Grade I listed main entrance building, visible on the
right. In early 2009 proposals were revealed that could see
a new station built at the site as part of a new high-speed
national link, but even if it were to go ahead it is unlikely
that any work will start for many years to come.

Another former GWR station, Moor Street (left) has
undergone a major renovation thanks in no small part to
the redevelopment of the Bullring shopping centre, which
lies next door. The station was built as a terminus for trains
coming from the east in order to help reduce the congestion
on the tunnel to Birmingham Snow Hill. This can be seen in
the top right of the image, with the lines to New Street
Station also visible as they pass under the platforms on the
middle right. Despite the closure of Snow Hill in 1972, Moor
Street remained open but gradually went into decline. The
development of the new Bullring from 2000-2003 was the
catalyst for the station's renaissance. The main entrance
buildings are Grade II listed and so would have survived
anyway, but an £11million investment has seen the station
restored to its 1930s glory, using many salvaged parts from
the original Snow Hill and the Tyseley Rail Museum. The
location of the station next to the Bullring (the famous
Selfridges store can be seen on the left) has seen
passenger numbers grow markedly to over 3.5 million in
2008/09, a figure that it probably wouldn't otherwise have
been able to reach.

Birmingham
Moor Street

Opened: 01/07/1909

Platforms: 5

Passengers (Ranking):
2008/9: 3,602,444 (91)
2007/8:   687,439 (540)
2006/7: 2,680,847 (121)
2005/6:   245,628 (930)
2004/5:   161,187 (1112)

Tyseley Loco Works

The works at Tyseley started life in July 1908 as a GWR steam depot, which consisted of a repair shop and two turntables within a large brick built shed. There was also a coal stage and a weighbridge amongst other facilities. Each of the turntables had a diameter of 65 feet with 28 engine roads. The surviving turntable and the 28 engine roads can be seen in the image above, albeit now outdoors. Today it forms part of the Tyseley Locomotive Works, a museum owned by the Birmingham Railway Museum Trust, which was a body set up to preserve and run steam locomotives. Amongst the museum's collection is also a good number of diesel and electric engines, many of which can be seen around the turntable. The museum's foundations lay in the purchasing of the GWR Steam Engine "Clun Castle" in 1966 by "7029 Clun Castle Ltd", a company set up specifically to save the engine. Needing

somewhere to maintain it, a site at Tyseley was found comprising of t old coal stage. Eventually, a new building would be built over the stag that would go on to form the workshop and shed of the Tyseley Museum. This can be seen in the centre of the image opposite (the g dog-legged building). The modern site is shown in its entirety on the opposite page. The museum occupies the middle section of the site, a is flanked on the left by the modern London Midland Traction Maintenance Depot, and on the right by the old carriage sidings that still in use today. The trust now regularly runs steam trips with some its restored rolling stock from the nearby Tyseley Station, which is ju off the image in the bottom right.

Blackburn

Opened: 03/06/1846

Platforms: 4

Passengers (Ranking):
2008/9: 1,162,930 (374)
2007/8: 1,132,415 (374)
2006/7: 1,051,142 (379)
2005/6:   982,355 (310)
2004/5:   930,144 (321)

The principal factor behind the building of a line to Blackburn was the opening of the station in nearby Preston in 1840. Plans to link the two towns were mooted, and these came to fruition when an act of parliament on June 6th 1844 granted permission for the line to be built. It would be known as the Blackburn & Preston Railway. The original station buildings lasted for 40 years before they were replaced between 1886-88 by the current booking hall and office complex. This was constructed by the Lancashire & Yorkshire Railway, and there was also a large covered canopy over the platforms. By the late 1990s the canopy had fallen into decline, and so a new modern design was constructed over the main island platform at a cost of £6million. The main feature of the new roof is a "Taroidal Blister" (the raised central dome), measuring 128ft long by 39ft wide and 13ft high. This in turn is connected to an adjoining 111½ ft long by 26ft barrel. Between them

the two structures allow light down onto the stairwells and platforms below. The new roof opened in 2001 and the booking office, which is Grade II listed, was retained and restored along with part of the origin canopy. At its largest the station had 9 platforms, including 5 bays, bu the station is now only half the physical size that is used to be. The easternmost island platform (right) is now gone and only the footprint remains, although it is still clearly visible as it is now overgrown with grass. The remains of the southern bay platforms can be seen in the centre bottom of the image.

Blackpool North

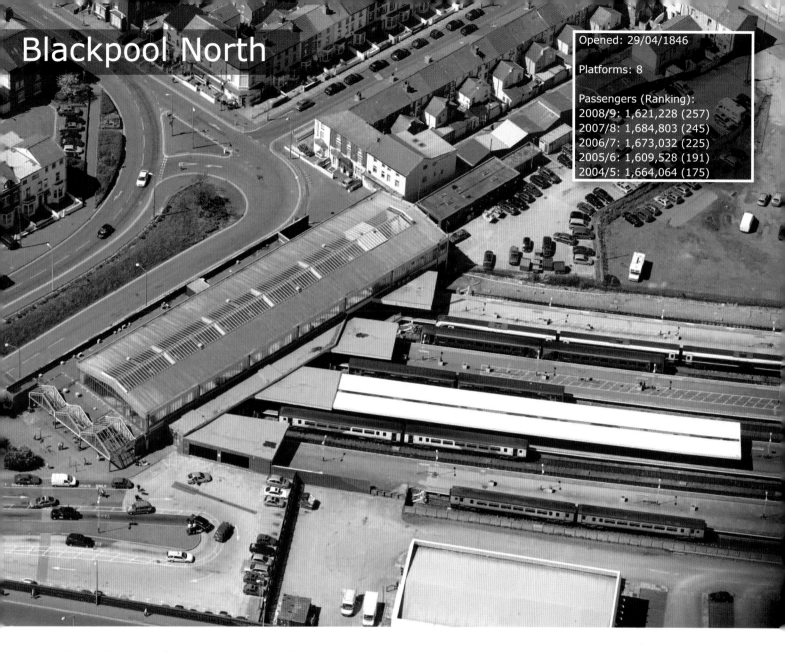

Opened: 29/04/1846

Platforms: 8

Passengers (Ranking):
2008/9: 1,621,228 (257)
2007/8: 1,684,803 (245)
2006/7: 1,673,032 (225)
2005/6: 1,609,528 (191)
2004/5: 1,664,064 (175)

he coming of the Railway was almost entirely responsible for the aking of Blackpool. When Blackpool North was opened on April 29th 846 (then known as Talbot Road Station) the town and the seaside uddenly became within easy reach of thousands of workers in ancashire and Yorkshire who would previously only have been able to each it by horse & cart or by foot. The subsequent huge influx of sitors led to Blackpool's rapid development into Britain's premier easide resort. Talbot Road, originally built by the Lancashire & orkshire Railway, was rebuilt in 1898, featuring two distinctive ctions. The first housed 6 platforms under the main double-arched ed and was used throughout the year, but the second, situated ghtly to the north east, had a further 10 platforms and was generally used for holidaymakers during the summer season, showing how popular the town was when the weather was fine. The entire station was rebuilt again in 1974 on the site of the old excursion platforms. The old shed was located just off the bottom left of the image, and is now the site of a combined supermarket and multi-storey car park. The modern station now houses 8 platforms and a fine and spacious concourse area that runs the length of the main building. The other main station in the town – Blackpool Central (originally "Hounds Hill" until 1878) - opened on April 4th 1863 on a site that would eventually be next to Blackpool Tower, which opened in 1893. At its height it had 14 platforms, but it was closed in early November 1964 leaving Blackpool North as the main entry point to the town and its attractions.

Bolton

Opened: 28/05/1838

Platforms: 4

Passengers (Ranking):
2008/9: 2,743,684 (133)
2007/8: 2,097,879 (190)
2006/7: 1,952,364 (189)
2005/6: 1,929,990 (151)
2004/5: 1,867,937 (152)

The Lancashire town of Bolton has played a major role in the history of the Railways. One of the first ever railways - the Bolton & Leigh Railway - opened in the town on July 1st 1828. Built by George and Robert Stephenson, it was a goods railway, 7 ½ miles in length, that was designed to be a rival to the canals for transporting of heavy goods produced in Bolton's factories. The terminus was at Bolton Great Moor Street, the first station in the town. The station featured 4 platforms and lasted until 1954, when it was closed. The Bolton & Leigh Railway was soon followed by the Manchester & Bolton Railway, construction of which started in 1831. It would run from Salford to Bolton, with the terminus here at Trinity Street (the street running above the station, on the left). The line was completed in May 1838, and the station was subsequently named Bolton Trinity Street. The old station building dated from the late 1890s. It was constructed by the Lancashire and Yorkshire Railway and contained an impressive clock tower at its northern end. The building was sadly demolished in 1987, but the clock tower was saved and re-sited. It can be seen in the bottom left of the photograph. A new entrance building was constructed to the north of Trinity Street (just out of shot on the left) in conjunction with a small bus station. This has led to the station being more commonly referred to as "Bolton Interchange", rather than simply Bolton.

Bradford Interchange & Bradford Forster Square

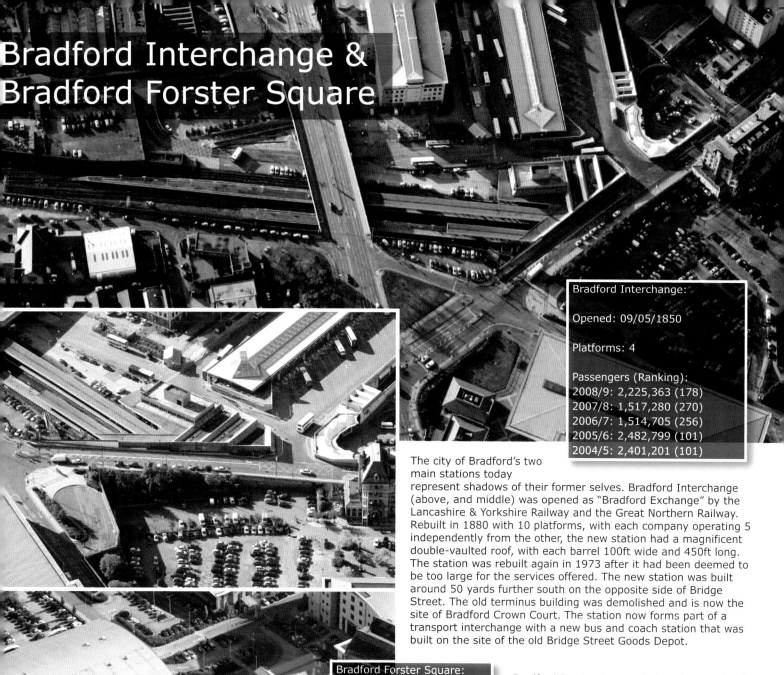

Bradford Interchange:

Opened: 09/05/1850

Platforms: 4

Passengers (Ranking):
2008/9: 2,225,363 (178)
2007/8: 1,517,280 (270)
2006/7: 1,514,705 (256)
2005/6: 2,482,799 (101)
2004/5: 2,401,201 (101)

The city of Bradford's two main stations today represent shadows of their former selves. Bradford Interchange (above, and middle) was opened as "Bradford Exchange" by the Lancashire & Yorkshire Railway and the Great Northern Railway. Rebuilt in 1880 with 10 platforms, with each company operating 5 independently from the other, the new station had a magnificent double-vaulted roof, with each barrel 100ft wide and 450ft long. The station was rebuilt again in 1973 after it had been deemed to be too large for the services offered. The new station was built around 50 yards further south on the opposite side of Bridge Street. The old terminus building was demolished and is now the site of Bradford Crown Court. The station now forms part of a transport interchange with a new bus and coach station that was built on the site of the old Bridge Street Goods Depot.

Bradford Forster Square:

Opened: 01/07/1846

Platforms: 3

Passengers (Ranking):
2008/9: 1,971,327 (212)
2007/8: 1,529,174 (268)
2006/7: 1,388,668 (284)
2005/6:   394,391 (667)
2004/5:   403,577 (630)

Bradford Forster Square (bottom) was a Leeds & Bradford Railway station opened in 1846. It was rebuilt several times, including in 1853 and 1890 by the Midland Railway, when the new station included an impressive Midland Hotel (which still stands) and 6 platforms. Known then as "Bradford", "Forster Square" was added to the name on June 2nd 1924. The station was rebuilt again in 1990 around 100 yards further north, but this time with only half as many platforms as before.

Today Bridgnorth is a world-famous steam heritage railway offering trips along the Severn Valley for thousands of tourists. The Severn Valley Railway was constructed between 1858 and 1861 from Hartlebury to Shrewsbury, a distance of 40 miles. The first train did not run until the following year, meaning that Bridgnorth did not officially open until 1862. The SVR was taken over by the Great Western Railway in July 1872, and in 1878 the line was extended to Kidderminster. The railway survived into 1963 when it was scheduled for closure due to falling passenger numbers. However, a group of railway enthusiasts got together in 1965 and managed to agree terms to purchase the line for £25,000, forming the Severn Valley Railway Society.

The society undertook a series of works to clear the lines of vegetation, and to preserve the stations and buildings along the route. The line reopened in 1970 with the first service to Hampton Loade running on May 23rd.

Today, Bridgnorth is the northern terminus for the Severn Valley Railway and it is also home to the main locomotive works, as can be seen in the larger photograph. The smaller image below shows the main platform, the station buildings and the signal box, which is to the left of the main building. The line now carries close to 250,000 passengers a year.

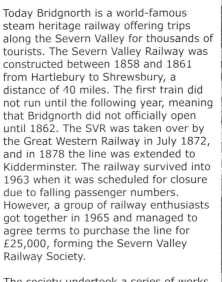

Brighton

This magnificent Grade II listed station was a creation of the London & Brighton Railway. The station opened on the line to Shoreham-By-Sea in 1840 and included 7 platforms and an impressive Italianate main station building that cost £12,000. The line to London Bridge opened a year later on September 21st, resulting in a huge influx of Victorian tourists seeking fun and relaxation by the sea. When Brighton was connected to London Victoria in October 1860, the number of passengers began to strain capacity at the station, and so a rebuild was undertaken in 1882, increasing the number of platforms to 10. The rebuild also saw the construction of the superb, three-span roof that remains to this day. It was constructed over the original roof, which was then taken down from the inside upon its completion. A new canopy over the entrance was also built at this time, which obscured the main station building, the top of which can be seen protruding through the glass in the picture. A huge restoration programme from 1997-2000 saw the roof re-glazed and returned to its original state. In the top right can be seen the white roof of Lovers Walk Traction and Rolling Stock Maintenance Depot.

Opened: 12/05/1840

Platforms: 8

Passengers (Ranking):
2008/9: 13,806,628 (24)
2007/8: 13,474,555 (22)
2006/7: 12,853,442 (22)
2005/6: 11,854,512 (20)
2004/5: 11,295,080 (21)

Bury

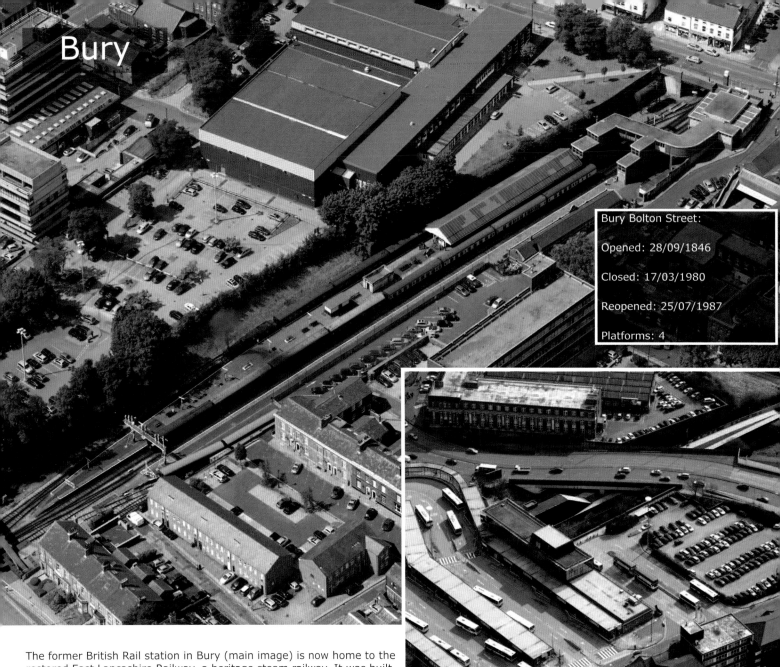

Bury Bolton Street:

Opened: 28/09/1846

Closed: 17/03/1980

Reopened: 25/07/1987

Platforms: 4

The former British Rail station in Bury (main image) is now home to the restored East Lancashire Railway, a heritage steam railway. It was built by the original ELR in 1846, later to become part of the Lancashire & Yorkshire Railway in 1859. The station was renamed as Bury Bolton Street in 1866, a name that survives to this day. The main Bury to Rawtenstall line remained open for passenger services until 1972, although the line was still utilised for goods until late 1980 when it was officially closed. Unlike many towns though, a new station was constructed elsewhere. Known as Bury Interchange (smaller image), this station opened along with new bus station a few hundred yards east of the old ELR terminus. However, rail services to this new station were to last for just over a decade, as Bury Interchange was converted to Metrolink use in 1991. Opened in June the following year, it now forms the northern most terminus of the Metrolink system. Bury Bolton Street would likely have been demolished altogether if it hadn't have been saved by the East Lancashire Preservation Society, who took up the challenge of restoring the line to its former glory. Established in 1968 to save a section of the line near Helmshore, the society instead switched its attentions to the Bury section, and were in a position to make a difference when the last freight train had rolled in 1980. The line officially reopened on July 25th 1987 between Bury and Ramsbottom, with the remainder of the track to Rawtenstall open by 1991. On average, over 120,000 people per year are now able to enjoy steam-powered trips on the restored railway.

Caerphilly

aerphilly has played an important role in the railways of South Wales. ven before it came to the town proper there had been railways in and round the area. The first of these was the 1836 Rhymney Tramway in he nearby town of Rhymney, which is now in the County Borough of aerphilly. The railways came closer in 1858 when the line to Nantgarw, ½ miles to the west, opened. It wasn't until 1868 that works started n the new Rhymney Railway that would bring a station right into the eart of the town. Along with a new hotel, the station connected the wn to Cardiff via the newly built 1.1 mile Cefn Onn tunnel, now also nown as the Caerphilly Tunnel. The station officially opened on April st 1871 when the first passenger service commenced. Caerphilly was nlarged to 5 platforms (4 through and 1 bay) in 1913 after passenger

demand left the old station unable to cope. By the 1970s however, the numbers using the station had decreased, and it was decided to rebuild again, this time to incorporate 2 platforms along with a bus interchange, which is visible next to the top platform. Opening in 1970, this is the layout that exists today at what is a small but perfectly comfortable station.

Opened: 01/04/1871

Platforms: 2

Passengers (Ranking):
2008/9: 598,214 (652)
2007/8: 606,461 (592)
2006/7: 608,934 (568)
2005/6: 599,509 (486)
2004/5: 620,269 (457)

Cardiff Central

Opened: 18/06/1850
Platforms: 7
Passengers (Ranking):
2008/9: 10,485,084 (30)
2007/8: 9,875,014 (29)
2006/7: 9,126,923 (29)
2005/6: 8,357,732 (24)
2004/5: 7,743,280 (26)

As the capital city of Wales, it is only to be expected that Cardiff has the largest and busiest station in the country. The latest figures show the station is now handling over 10 million passengers per year, a figure that continues to grow. It was opened by the South Wales Railway in 1850 and has undergone several periods of change over the years. It was first rebuilt in the late 1880s when the junction to Clarence Road Station was constructed to allow goods traffic to reach the Glamorgan Canal Company's warehouses further down the line. The site of the junction can still be seen on the middle right of the photograph, following the path of the road next to the white building with the pitched roof. There is also still a short spur of track in situ, just about visible at the very foot of the picture. The creation of this junction would ultimately lead to a second, separate station being constructed along the new spur. This was known as Riverside Junction Station, which

opened in September 1882, with passenger services commencing on April 2nd 1894. The station featured 3 platforms, including an island on the southern side. After the Great Western Railway took over the SWR, Cardiff General (as it had been known since 1922) was rebuilt again from 1931-1933, which included lengthening the platforms on the main station as well as those on the Riverside Junction Station. The two stations were also connected by a new building (the aforementioned white building). Nowadays there is no visible trace of Riverside Station. It was only incorporated into Cardiff General late in October 1940, but had closed by March 1964. The lines out to Clarence Road were lifted soon afterwards, but the station remained in use as a parcel dock for several years. Since May 1973 the station has been known as "Cardiff Central".

Cardiff Canton T.M.D.

Situated around 500 yards directly west of Cardiff Central is Canton Traction Maintenance Depot. There has been a major depot on this site since June 1882, when a steam locomotive depot was opened by the South Wales Railway. Facilities at the original depot included a 240ft long maintenance shed, which was followed by a 28-road turntable in 1897. After the GWR took over the site operations peaked in the mid 1920s, but the maintenance of steam locomotives continued up until the early 1960s. The depot was forced to close in 1962, being demolished by the middle of the next year, but a new DMU depot was to be constructed in its place. The new depot included a large main shed (on the right) and a smaller servicing shed (middle). Just in front of the servicing shed is a locomotive washing shed, and on the right of the main shed are the main sidings.

Carlisle Citadel

The station at Carlisle is one of the most impressive in the country, and since November 1972 has been afforded Grade II* listed status. Designed by architect Sir William Tite, the station was opened in 1847 for the Lancaster & Carlisle Railway and the Caledonian Railway. It was operated by both companies as a joint station, but would also be home to services from the Maryport & Carlisle Railway and the Newcastle & Carlisle Railway. Both of these railways previously used Carlisle London Road Station, which opened on July 19th 1836 on a site just to the south east of the current station. The M&CR would use Citadel for its services once it was completed, leaving just the N&CR to operate out of London Road until it finally closed on January 1st 1863, later becoming a large goods depot. The main façade Of Carlisle Station is built in sandstone and features an elegant, octagonal clock tower in the centre, along with a five-bay porte-cochere (a porch large enough for vehicles), which is just visible to the left of the clock tower. The station was extended in 1879-80 and featured an enormous roof covering almost 6 acres. This was subsequently cut back in size between 1957-58 and later demolished completely. Looking at the image, we can see a large freestanding wall (which itself is Grade II listed) on the far side of the station, and also a section of wall on the near right side. This was the extent of the 1879 roof over all of the platforms and these walls were part of the supporting structure. The station today is a major stop on the West Coast Main Line, and the last port of call in England for London to Glasgow services.

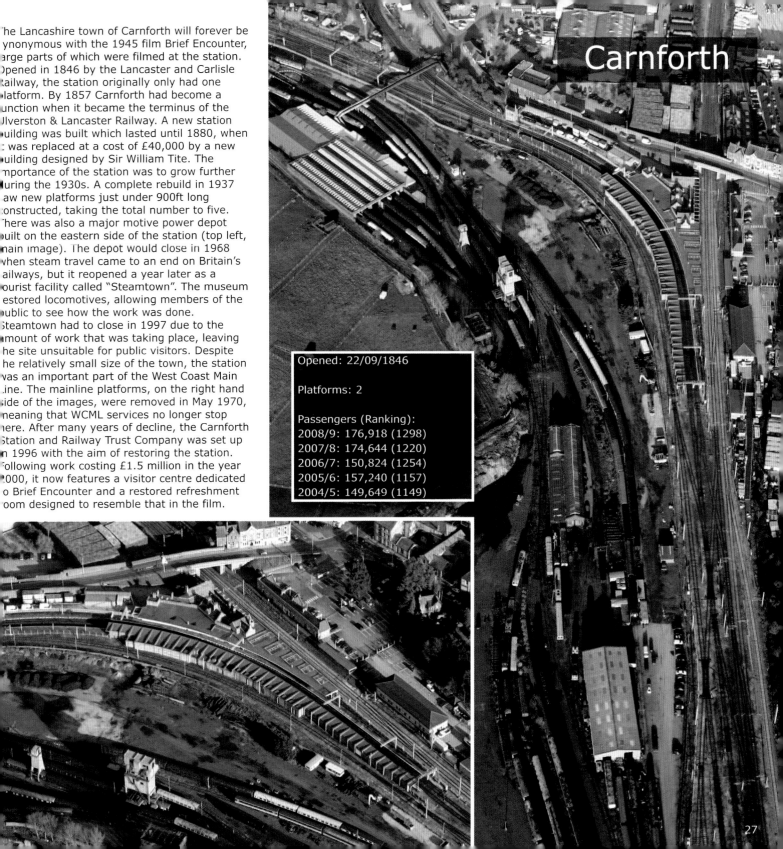

The Lancashire town of Carnforth will forever be synonymous with the 1945 film Brief Encounter, large parts of which were filmed at the station. Opened in 1846 by the Lancaster and Carlisle Railway, the station originally only had one platform. By 1857 Carnforth had become a junction when it became the terminus of the Ulverston & Lancaster Railway. A new station building was built which lasted until 1880, when it was replaced at a cost of £40,000 by a new building designed by Sir William Tite. The importance of the station was to grow further during the 1930s. A complete rebuild in 1937 saw new platforms just under 900ft long constructed, taking the total number to five. There was also a major motive power depot built on the eastern side of the station (top left, main image). The depot would close in 1968 when steam travel came to an end on Britain's railways, but it reopened a year later as a tourist facility called "Steamtown". The museum restored locomotives, allowing members of the public to see how the work was done. Steamtown had to close in 1997 due to the amount of work that was taking place, leaving the site unsuitable for public visitors. Despite the relatively small size of the town, the station was an important part of the West Coast Main Line. The mainline platforms, on the right hand side of the images, were removed in May 1970, meaning that WCML services no longer stop here. After many years of decline, the Carnforth Station and Railway Trust Company was set up in 1996 with the aim of restoring the station. Following work costing £1.5 million in the year 2000, it now features a visitor centre dedicated to Brief Encounter and a restored refreshment room designed to resemble that in the film.

Opened: 22/09/1846

Platforms: 2

Passengers (Ranking):
2008/9: 176,918 (1298)
2007/8: 174,644 (1220)
2006/7: 150,824 (1254)
2005/6: 157,240 (1157)
2004/5: 149,649 (1149)

Cheltenham Spa

Opened: 24/06/1840

Platforms: 2

Passengers (Ranking):
2008/9: 1,529,004 (281)
2007/8: 1,338,855 (315)
2006/7: 1,206,187 (326)
2005/6: 1,128,845 (268)
2004/5: 1,036,744 (287)

Spa Station is now the main station in the elegant town of Cheltenham. Built by the Birmingham & Gloucester Railway, the station was to open in 1840 as Lansdown Station. At one point there were seven stations in or around the vicinity of Cheltenham, but following the closures of the 1960s associated with Dr Beeching, Spa Station was to be the last one standing. More recently, however, Cheltenham Racecourse Station was reopened in 2003, meaning there are now two operational stations in the area. Like so many buildings in the town, the main station building is resplendent in white limestone, echoing the Regency character of many of the buildings on the town's streets. It was designed by Samuel Whitfield Daukes, who was chief architect for the Birmingham & Gloucester Railway and who would go on to design many other prominent buildings in the town. The biggest change to the station occurred in 1965 when the platforms were lengthened to accommodate larger trains travelling to and from London. One very famous visitor was Queen Victoria, who travelled through the station in October 1849. The Royal train did not stop, but it slowed in order to allow the gathered hordes of people the chance to get a brief glimpse of the Monarch, with people packed several layers deep on both the platforms and the old footbridge.

Chester

Opened: 01/08/1848		
Platforms: 8		
Passengers (Ranking):		
2008/9: 2,829,358	(127)	
2007/8: 2,607,835	(140)	
2006/7: 2,440,874	(141)	
2005/6: 2,336,893	(112)	
2004/5: 2,239,061	(115)	

This fine station was opened in 1848 as a joint project by several railway companies. It replaced earlier stations in the city built by the Chester & Birkenhead Railway (September 1840), and the Chester & Crewe Railway (October 1840). Following completion of the line to Holyhead in 1848 by the Chester & Holyhead Railway, the city was starting to become an important junction and it was soon clear that a new joint station would be required in order to handle the number of passengers. Designed by the prominent railway architect Francis Thompson, who worked with Robert Stephenson on many of his lines, the magnificent main building was built in Italianate style with impressive end pavilions.

A second large station in the city was opened for goods in 1874 – Chester Northgate. When passengers were admitted the following year, the much larger 1848 station changed its name to "Chester General" in order to help differentiate between the two. This name lasted until 1969. Recently, £11 million has been spent regenerating and restoring the Grade II* listed main building, including new glazing in the roof, repairs to the façade and improvements to customer facilities. To the west of the station there is a DMU depot and wagon works (below). Throughout its existence this has been a major stabling and maintenance point on the North Wales main line, and for the lines into Shropshire. It is now known simply as "Chester Diesel Depot".

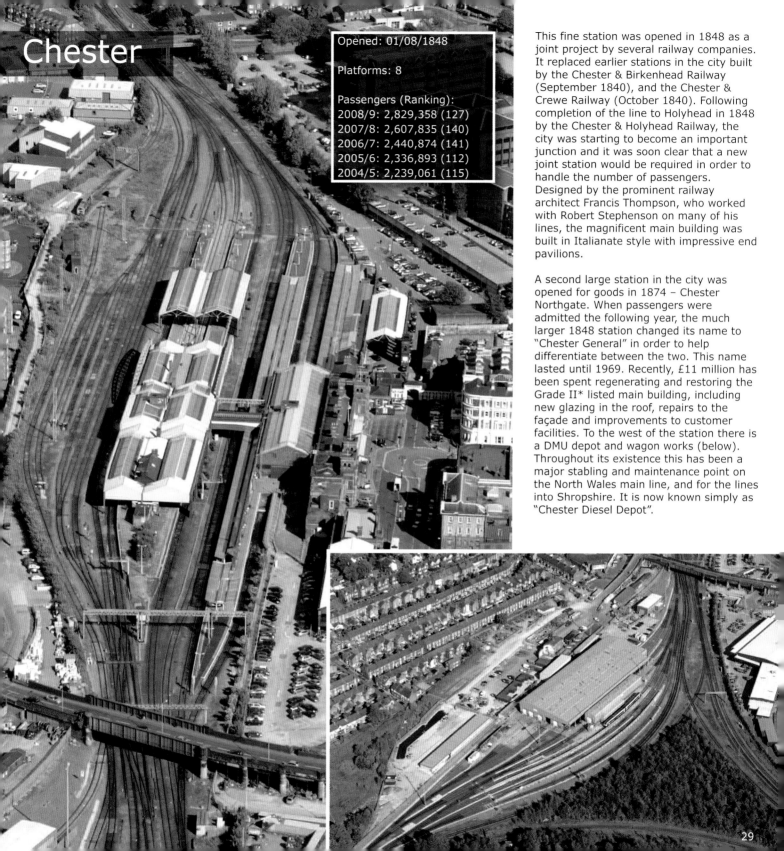

Coventry

Opened: 09/04/1838

Platforms: 4

Passengers (Ranking):
2008/9: 4,519,856 (70)
2007/8: 3,039,543 (106)
2006/7: 2,874,928 (107)
2005/6: 2,719,034 (94)
2004/5: 2,359,641 (105)

Coventry station is held up as a classic of late 1950s, early 1960s architecture. When work on the current station started in 1959 the platforms and buildings had remained almost untouched for over 120 years. As a testament to the quality of the design, in 1995 the station attained Grade II listed status, being recognised for the main booking hall and the platform buildings. English Heritage describes the design as "Outstanding architecturally, particularly for its spatial qualities and detailing". The original station was opened by the London & Birmingham Railway, but it was rebuilt within two years at a site only 900ft further east down the track due to the shortness of the platforms. The original station had only two platforms with two through lines through the centre, but the new station comprised 4 platforms and overhead electric cables in anticipation of the electrification of the line through the city in 1966. Coventry was also an important goods site. A goods shed and yard was built by the London & Birmingham Railway when the first station was constructed, just a hundred yards or so to the left of the above photograph. Today, nothing remains of the yard, and the site is now a large retail park. Interestingly, the number of passengers has almost doubled in the last 5 years despite the station being relatively small for such a large city.

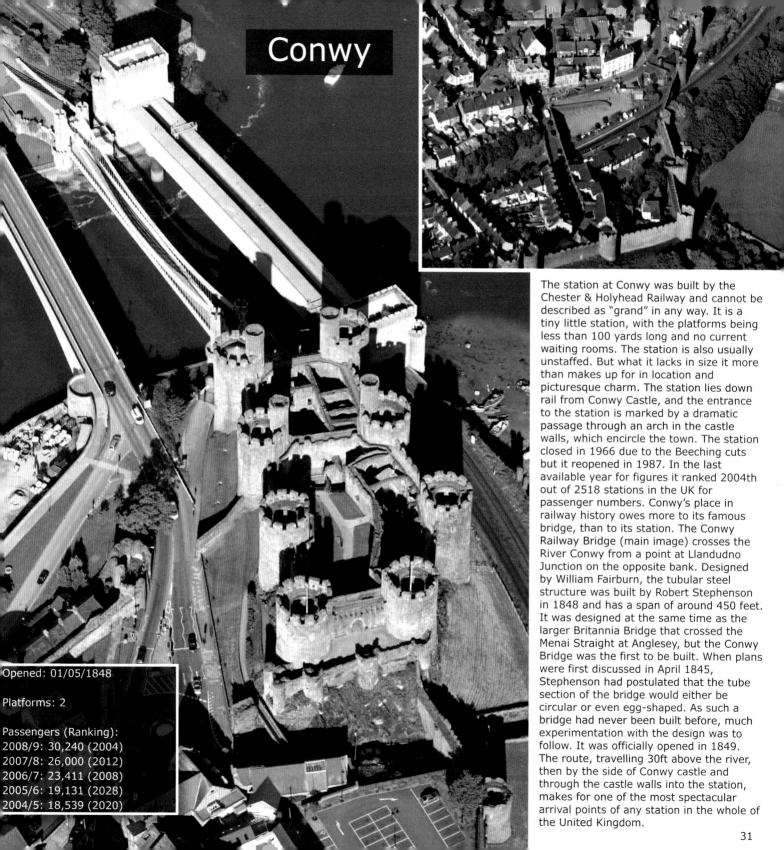

Conwy

The station at Conwy was built by the Chester & Holyhead Railway and cannot be described as "grand" in any way. It is a tiny little station, with the platforms being less than 100 yards long and no current waiting rooms. The station is also usually unstaffed. But what it lacks in size it more than makes up for in location and picturesque charm. The station lies down rail from Conwy Castle, and the entrance to the station is marked by a dramatic passage through an arch in the castle walls, which encircle the town. The station closed in 1966 due to the Beeching cuts but it reopened in 1987. In the last available year for figures it ranked 2004th out of 2518 stations in the UK for passenger numbers. Conwy's place in railway history owes more to its famous bridge, than to its station. The Conwy Railway Bridge (main image) crosses the River Conwy from a point at Llandudno Junction on the opposite bank. Designed by William Fairburn, the tubular steel structure was built by Robert Stephenson in 1848 and has a span of around 450 feet. It was designed at the same time as the larger Britannia Bridge that crossed the Menai Straight at Anglesey, but the Conwy Bridge was the first to be built. When plans were first discussed in April 1845, Stephenson had postulated that the tube section of the bridge would either be circular or even egg-shaped. As such a bridge had never been built before, much experimentation with the design was to follow. It was officially opened in 1849. The route, travelling 30ft above the river, then by the side of Conwy castle and through the castle walls into the station, makes for one of the most spectacular arrival points of any station in the whole of the United Kingdom.

Opened: 01/05/1848

Platforms: 2

Passengers (Ranking):
2008/9: 30,240 (2004)
2007/8: 26,000 (2012)
2006/7: 23,411 (2008)
2005/6: 19,131 (2028)
2004/5: 18,539 (2020)

Crewe

There are many places, both large and small in Great Britain, that are Railway towns, but Crewe is *the* great railway town. As both a major junction and a major manufacturing centre, Crewe has almost no equal in the history of the UK's railways, or the world's. Indeed, so important was the railway that the town is named after the station and not the other war around, as the town did not exist before the railway came. The station was built as a result of the opening of the Grand Junction Railway that linked the existing Liverpool and Manchester Railway with the London and Birmingham Railway. Before its construction the land was fields belonging to the Earl of Crewe, but within a few years the site had grown dramatically into a major railway hub with six converging lines. The Chester & Crewe Railway opened in October 1840, and this was followed by the Manchester & Birmingham Railway in August 1842. The North Staffordshire Railway (October 1848) and the Crewe & Shrewsbury Railway (September 1858) were

the remaining lines to be added. All six remain open and today the station is still one of the busiest junctions on the West Coast Main Line. Despite still being a small town, the scale of the station is vast. Of particular interest is the Crewe Arms Hotel, (bottom left, opposite page) which opened in 1838 and is believed to be the world's first railway hotel. On the far side of the station we can see four separate tracks with no platforms. These were added in the late 19th century so that goods traffic could avoid the main station and free-up capacity. Crewe's history with the railways has led to the building of the Crewe Heritage Centre (opposite, top right), on the site of the old loco works. Opened in 1987 to coincide with the 150th anniversary of the station, visitors can learn all about the building and growth of Crewe, and also see some of the rolling stock. Pride of place goes to the APT (Advanced Passenger Train), which is visible in the foreground.

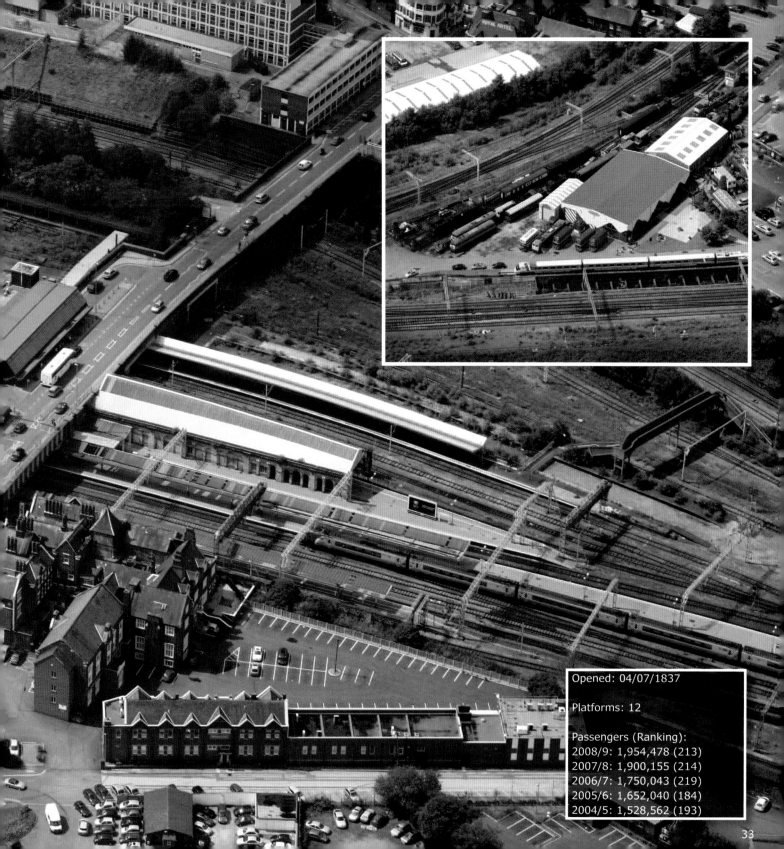

Opened: 04/07/1837

Platforms: 12

Passengers (Ranking):
2008/9: 1,954,478 (213)
2007/8: 1,900,155 (214)
2006/7: 1,750,043 (219)
2005/6: 1,652,040 (184)
2004/5: 1,528,562 (193)

Crewe Loco Works & Depots

The importance of the founding of Crewe Locomotive Works can be summed up by the effect it had on the population of the town. When Crewe Station opened in 1837 there was no town of Crewe, merely a couple of hamlets named Monks Coppenhall where the station had been built, and Church Coppenhall to the north. The population of Monks Coppenhall in 1841 was recorded as little more than 100. By 1891 the town of Crewe had a population of 44,800, with over 8,000 directly employed by the locomotive works. In 1843 the Grand Junction Railway were to open the first works just to the north of the station, replacing their existing factory at Edge Hill in Liverpool. Along with the works came houses and public facilities for the workers, many of whom had been employed at Edge Hill. The great railway engineer Joesph Locke is the man credited with the laying out of the town. It was his grouping of railway cottages built to house those workers that can be considered the first major settlement. The rest of the town soon sprang up around it, including the town hall in 1847. The GJR works was built on a 30-acre site just to the north of the station between the Chester & Warrington Lines. The first steam engine rolled off the production line in 1843, one of 7,331 that it would produce in its lifetime. It was the largest and most advanced railway works in the world, and at its height it would employ well over 10,000 people. The site would eventually spread over 1½ miles westward along the side of the Chester Branch Line, covering a total of 137 acres. The left image is taken from the very west of the site, and is looking back down the Chester line towards Crewe Station. On the right is the Crewe Electric Traction Maintenance Depot, which despite being on the southern side of the tracks was also part of the site, and was accessed via a flat crossing. Today, much of the land occupied by the loco works has been sold off for redevelopment, with current work focusing on maintenance, rather than construction.

Basford Hall Freight Yard (above) is sited around a mile south of Crewe station. It opened in 1901 and is used for general stabling and shunting of both freight wagons and locomotives. The site has been identified as a possible location for a new Crewe Station by Network Rail. In 2007 they outlined claims that capacity at the existing station would be reached within the next 15 years, and so a replacement would be required. As yet, there are no official plans for any new station on this site, and the existing Crewe Station is likely to remain in place for a long time yet. In the top left of the image can be seen the modern LNWR maintenance depot, which was acquired by Arriva in 2008. Although the company bears the name of the London & North Western it was only founded in 1993 by the rail enthusiast & music producer Pete Waterman. Slightly further north on the western side of the track is the Crewe diesel traction maintenance depot (left).

Darlington Bank Top

Opened: 01/07/1887
Platforms: 4
Passengers (Ranking):
2008/9: 2,184,436 (187)
2007/8: 2,099,480 (189)
2006/7: 2,013,516 (181)
2005/6: 1,906,131 (153)
2004/5: 1,795,683 (159)

Darlington's place in railway history is assured thanks to the Stockton & Darlington Railway, the world's first steam railway. It was constructed in 1825 along with a branch line to Shildon, and contained a total of 26 miles of track. Much of the original site in Darlington is now a museum called "Head of Steam", and is built around North Road Station in the north of the town. Exhibits include George Stephenson's "Locomotion No. 1", the first passenger engine on the line. The station building is Grade II* listed and is still used for local services. The importance of North Road began to fall with the building of the first Bank Top station in 1841 as part of the Newcastle to York line. It was opened by the Great North of England Railway on a section of mineral (coal) track built by the Stockton & Darlington Railway. Although it was only a temporary stop, demand would eventually see a rebuild in 1860, followed by a completely new station slightly down the line in 1887, which is the station that exists today. Designed by William Bell for the North Eastern Railway (the successor to the S&DR), the station features wide, spacious platforms under a triple-arched barrel roof. Bank Top's station buildings have also been Grade II* listed, since September 1977. Built of red brick, the main entrance is dominated by an imposing central clock tower with a crested pyramidal roof (on the far side), which can be seen for miles around. The station is now extremely busy, with over 2 million passengers per year. The avoiding freight lines on the eastern side of the station (bottom) were once the site of 14 rail sidings used for goods. Much of this site is now occupied by the station car park.

Dewsbury

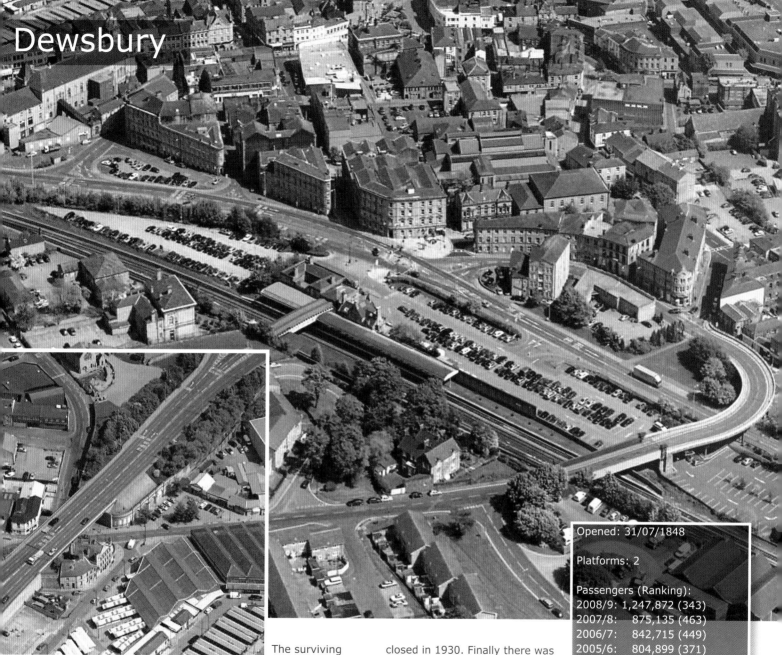

The surviving station in ewsbury was opened in July 1848 by the London & North Western ailway, with the first passenger services commencing on September 3th. It was renamed "Dewsbury Wellington Road" in 1924 before everting back to simply "Dewsbury" in 1969. The main building cost 5,597 to construct and since November 1977 has been Grade II listed ong with the rest of the station. At one point there were four stations the town. Along with Wellington Road there was Thornhill, which was ened by the Lancashire & Yorkshire Railway. It was the first station to en on the outskirts of town, and closed in 1961. Dewsbury Market ace, also a L&YR station, opened next to the town hall in 1866. It closed in 1930. Finally there was Dewsbury Central. Central station was opened in 1880 by the Great Northern Railway, with services to Leeds, Bradford, Wakefield and London King's Cross. It was a grand terminus station with a large island platform and multi-span roof with 15 arches in total. The station closed in 1964 but its remains are still prominent (smaller image), as the entrances to the station were incorporated into the town's new ring road in 1985. The station hotel is still standing on the opposite side of the road. The bridge carrying the new road sits upon some of the original rail bridge's stone plinths, which are still visible at street level.

Didcot Parkway & Didcot Railway Centre

Didcot Station was opened by the Great Western Railway in 1844, with Brunel himself designing the buildings. The GWR line had been extended from Reading through the town 5 years earlier, but it was the construction of the branch line to Oxford that would eventually lead to the station being built. Like in many towns, the railway brought a population boom, and the previously tiny village began a rapid expansion. The name of the station remained the same until 1985 when it was renamed "Didcot Parkway", when Park & Ride facilities were introduced. Didcot is also the home of the Didcot Railway Centre, built on the site of the GWR works in between some of the main line tracks. It is based around the original GWR engine shed which dates from 1932, which can be seen in the very centre of the main picture (left). The centre is run by the Great Western Society who took charge of the site in 1967 with the aim of preserving and restoring GWR steam engines. The centre boasts its own small stations between short runs of track, as well as a large 200ft carriage and wagon display shed and turntable (opposite page, bottom left). The turntable has a length of 70 feet and is built on the site of the original 1932 GWR turntable, which had been removed prior to 1967. Also of interest is the coal stage (opposite, bottom right), which was used for supplying locomotives with coal and water when they had run out of steam.

Opened: 12/06/1844

Platforms: 5

Passengers (Ranking):
2008/9: 2,456,384 (163)
2007/8: 2,416,635 (159)
2006/7: 2,290,949 (155)
2005/6: 2,175,689 (120)
2004/5: 2,181,924 (120)

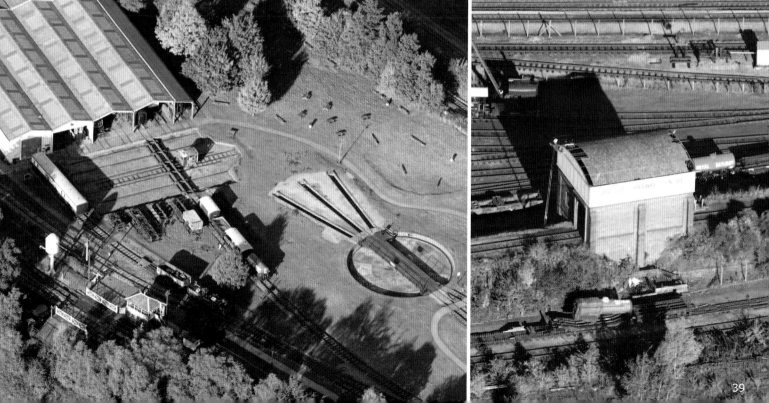

Doncaster

The line into Doncaster was built by the Great Northern Railway in 1848, and was to be the catalyst for the town becoming a major railway centre. The station was well placed for transporting coal from the Yorkshire collieries, and a number of branch lines were soon converging on the site of the new station, with fierce competition from all of the main players in the industry, including the Lancashire & Yorkshire Railway, the Midland and the North Eastern railways. It wasn't until a few years later, in 1851, that the seeds for Doncaster's future were sown, when the GNR opted to build a major works on the adjacent 11-acre site. Opening in 1853, the works initially only dealt with repairing of locomotives, but the decision was taken to manufacture them in April 1867. Known throughout the land and even throughout the world, "The Plant", as the works were fondly known, would go on to produce some of the most remarkable steam engines ever

built. The most famous of these is undoubtedly The Mallard, which still holds the world steam locomotive speed record at 126mph, which it set in July 1938. It also built The Flying Scotsman, the first locomotive to break the 100mph barrier. Eventually the site would expand to over 200 acres. At the foot of the large image some of the buildings can be seen. The footbridge over the station led workers directly to The Plant. The brick building to the right is the Central Drawing Office, and behind this at the very foot of the image is the Carriage Building Shop and Carriage Paint Shop complex. The smaller image offers a wider view of the remaining buildings.

Opened: 07/09/1848

Platforms: 8

Passengers (Ranking):
2008/9: 3,780,314 (86)
2007/8: 2,903,339 (116)
2006/7: 2,790,811 (112)
2005/6: 2,837,400 (90)
2004/5: 2,772,500 (92)

Dover Priory

Opened: 22/07/1861

Platforms: 3

Passengers (Ranking):
2008/9: 945,392 (467)
2007/8: 960,407 (423)
2006/7: 923,163 (413)
2005/6: 860,722 (348)
2004/5: 902,190 (329)

When Dover Priory station opened it was the second in Dover after Dover Town (July 1844). It was initially a temporary terminus built by the London, Chatham and Dover Railway, and would not become a through station until November that year when the line was extended through a tunnel to the docks and Dover Harbour Station. This allowed for journeys directly to the coast and to ferry departure points. Dover Harbour lasted until 1927, but by that time a new station had been built on Admiralty Pier called Dover Marine (below). The station was almost ready for use in 1914, leading to the closure of the old and small Dover Admiralty Pier Station (1861-August 1914), but the outbreak of The Great War led to it being used for military purposes only until 1919. Built on land reclaimed from the sea by dumping chalk deposits and blocks of concrete, Dover Marine was an impressive terminus directly by the sea. The new station was fully enclosed to protect from the elements, and featured 4 platforms. The station closed in 1994 following the opening of the Channel Tunnel, which would render it redundant. Whilst the tracks had been removed by 1996, the station building was retained having become a Grade II listed building in June 1989. It is now an elegant cruise terminal in Dover's western docks, and is used by many prominent cruise companies throughout the year.

Opened: 02/01/1915 *(Military Use)*
           18/01/1919 *(Public Use)*

Closed: 25/09/1994

Platforms: 4

Dover Marine (disused)

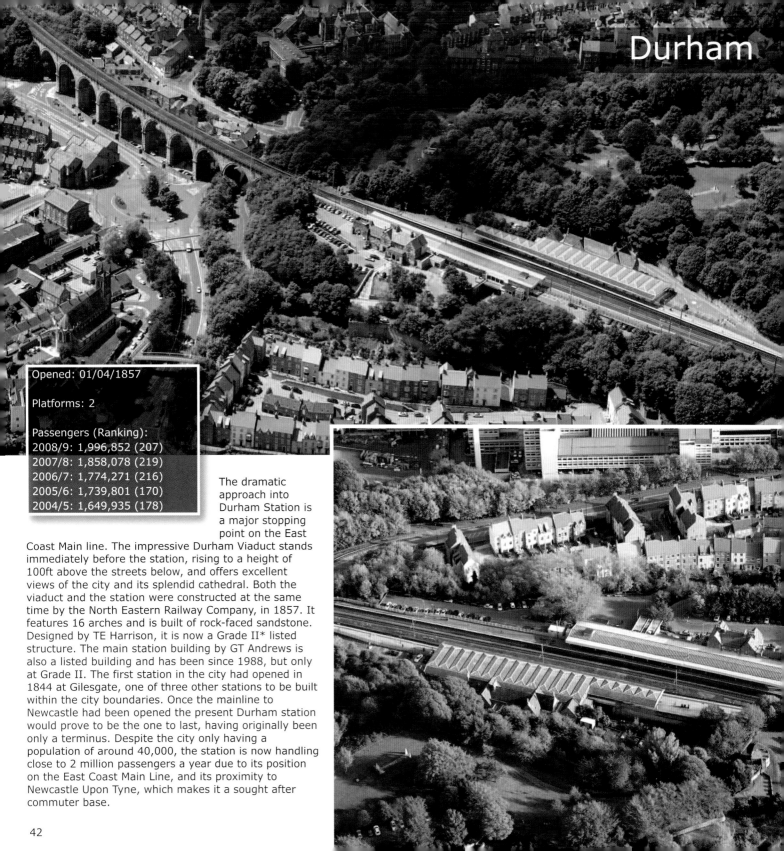

Opened: 01/04/1857

Platforms: 2

Passengers (Ranking):
2008/9: 1,996,852 (207)
2007/8: 1,858,078 (219)
2006/7: 1,774,271 (216)
2005/6: 1,739,801 (170)
2004/5: 1,649,935 (178)

The dramatic approach into Durham Station is a major stopping point on the East Coast Main line. The impressive Durham Viaduct stands immediately before the station, rising to a height of 100ft above the streets below, and offers excellent views of the city and its splendid cathedral. Both the viaduct and the station were constructed at the same time by the North Eastern Railway Company, in 1857. It features 16 arches and is built of rock-faced sandstone. Designed by TE Harrison, it is now a Grade II* listed structure. The main station building by GT Andrews is also a listed building and has been since 1988, but only at Grade II. The first station in the city had opened in 1844 at Gilesgate, one of three other stations to be built within the city boundaries. Once the mainline to Newcastle had been opened the present Durham station would prove to be the one to last, having originally been only a terminus. Despite the city only having a population of around 40,000, the station is now handling close to 2 million passengers a year due to its position on the East Coast Main Line, and its proximity to Newcastle Upon Tyne, which makes it a sought after commuter base.

Eastbourne

Opened: 14/05/1849

Platforms: 3

Passengers (Ranking):
2008/9: 3,513,854 (96)
2007/8: 3,545,125 (90)
2006/7: 3,272,506 (90)
2005/6: 3,080,715 (84)
2004/5: 3,065,020 (81)

The original station on this site was opened by the London, Brighton & South Coast Railway as a branch line off the Brighton to Hastings route in 1849. At the time of its construction there was no large built-up area around Eastbourne, just a series of small hamlets. Like elsewhere on the coast, the arrival of the railways led to the development of the town into a major seaside resort. The popularity of Eastbourne would see the station rebuilt in 1866 and again in 1886 into the one that stands today. Designed by LB&SCR engineer FD Bannister, the station is now a Grade II listed building. Originally it had 4 platforms, but today it has only three. The line of the track into the fourth platform can still be traced on the right hand side of the picture, where there is now a thin line of greenery just next to the existing platform. As can be seen in the picture, in the top left there are a few railway sidings still in use. These lines led to a small goods shed and coal depot which is now covered by the station car park. The goods shed was eventually extended to cover the whole of this site and suffered from bomb damage in 1941 during World War Two. Today the station handles an impressive number of passengers (over 3.5 million), and makes for an excellent gateway to the south coast.

Edinburgh Waverley

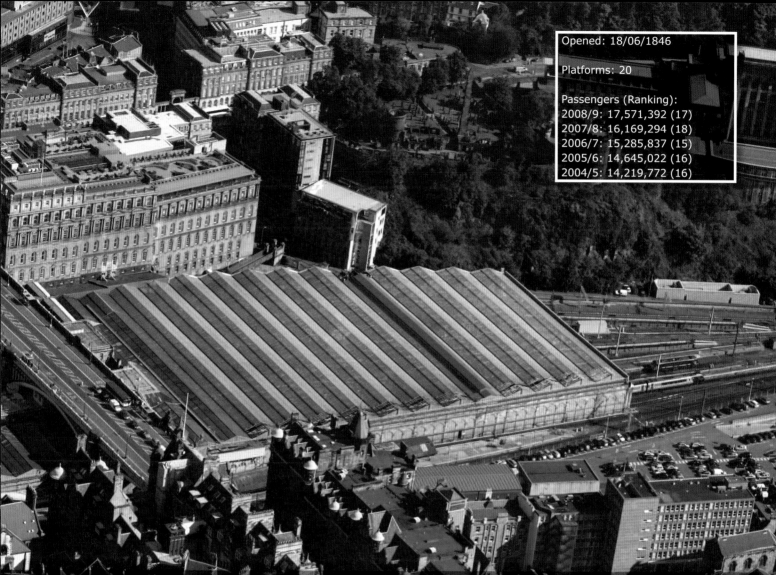

Opened: 18/06/1846

Platforms: 20

Passengers (Ranking):
2008/9: 17,571,392 (17)
2007/8: 16,169,294 (18)
2006/7: 15,285,837 (15)
2005/6: 14,645,022 (16)
2004/5: 14,219,772 (16)

Scotland's capital city is the terminus for the East Coast Main Line for journeys from London King's Cross. From the air the arrival point is one of the most impressive in the whole of the UK. The huge station sits in a small valley next to the world famous Princes Street, acting as a link between the Old Town in the east and the New Town in the west. This image shows the huge scale of the station buildings. Covering over 24 acres, it is the second largest station in Great Britain in area, behind only London Waterloo, and the roof alone covers over 34,000 square feet. The two bridges across the station help give an idea as to its sunken level, with Waverley Bridge on the left and North Bridge in the middle. The first station on this site was known as North Bridge Station and was the main forerunner to Waverley. It was opened in June 1846 by the North British Railway, with the lines passing through the arches of the old North Bridge, which stood from 1763 until 1896. It was a relatively small station, meaning there was enough room for two rival stations to be built immediately next to it. The first of these was General Station, which opened just over six weeks later on August 1st and was built by the Edinburgh & Glasgow Railway. The third was Canal Street, which was completed by May 17th 1847 and was built at

a right angle to North Bridge, facing north. This was an Edinburgh, Leith and Granton Railway station. Today it lies under the site of Waverley Market, which has now been redeveloped as Princes Mall Shopping Centre (between Waverley Bridge and the Balmoral Hotel, top centre). As North Bridge was the principal of the three stations, it can be said that this was, in effect, the station that exists today. The name of "Waverley Station" is thought to have been given as a description to all three either in 1854 or 1866, depending on the sources. Canal Street was finally closed in May 1868 when the whole site was redeveloped as one new station. It was to undergo another major redevelopment by the North British Railway from 1892-1902, resulting in the station that stands today. The number of platforms was extended to 19, and other new features included the magnificent booking hall, with its tiled mosaic floor, glass cupola and wooden booking office. The Balmoral Hotel was originally the North British Hotel, having been opened by the NBR in October 1902, and features a 190ft clock tower facing onto Princes Street. Today the station has 20 platforms, but platforms 5 and 6 are generally only used for stabling of engines.

Haymarket & Haymarket T.M.D.

Haymarket Station (inset) is Edinburgh's second station, and is situated around a mile west of Waverley. It predates the original North Bridge station by four years, opening in February 1842 as the terminus for the Edinburgh & Glasgow Railway, with services running to Glasgow Queen Street. It wasn't until the Haymarket tunnels were constructed by the North British Railway that the line was connected into the heart of the city. The entrances to the tunnels are visible at the top of the image. Originally the station had 4 platforms, but a new bay platform opened in December 2006, visible on the left of the image. The main image shows Haymarket Traction Maintenance Depot, which is a mile further west. This was another NBR facility and originally featured a large locomotive shed on the site of the current main shed, and a turntable at the eastern end. The depot is now used for the maintenance of DMUs and was recently refurbished at a cost of £6.7 million. A new shed was built at the eastern end (top right) that will enable both light and heavy maintenance works to take place. The new buildings were opened on February 13th 2007.

Opened: 21/02/1842

Platforms: 5

Passengers (Ranking):
2008/9: 1,742,820 (238)
2007/8: 1,607,354 (258)
2006/7: 1,620,102 (237)
2005/6: 1,658,339 (183)
2004/5: 1,571,356 (188)

The Forth Bridge

Perhaps *the* great feat of Victorian Engineering, The Forth Bridge has come to be one of the symbols of modern Scotland. Designed by Sir John Fowler and Sir Benjamin Baker, the bridge allows rail services from Fife and the north to reach the capital city over the Firth of Forth. At 8,296 feet long (2765 ⅓ yards, or 1.57 miles) it is the longest cantilevered railway bridge in the world, and the second longest cantilevered bridge of any kind. Work started on the bridge in 1883 by the Glasgow based Sir William Arrol & Co, who would go on to build Tower Bridge in London (1894) and the new North Bridge over Waverley Station (1897). Over 4,500 men worked on it's construction for seven years, finally seeing it open in March 1890. At its highest point the bridge reaches 330ft and clears the water below at around 150ft. At its lowest, the supports reach down 91ft into the waters of the Forth. The total cost of the project when completed was a huge £3.2 million, but an even heavier price had been paid by then. During its construction 57 men were recorded as having died (the total figure may well actually be closer to 100), and almost 500 were injured. The plans for the bridge were originally in the hands of engineer Sir Thomas Bouch, who had worked for the North British Railway and had designed parts of Waverley Station. Work on his design had actually commenced when disaster struck one of his existing works, the Tay Bridge, on December 28th 1879. The bridge collapsed during a storm taking a locomotive and its 75 passengers with it. After an enquiry it was found that the bridge contained many engineering defects, and so Bouch was stripped of his responsibility on the Forth Bridge project. The new Forth Bridge has had no such problems, although it does require a constant programme of maintenance. On the left can be seen the Forth Road Bridge, which opened in September 1964, and beyond the two bridges are the Ochil Hills.

Exeter Central

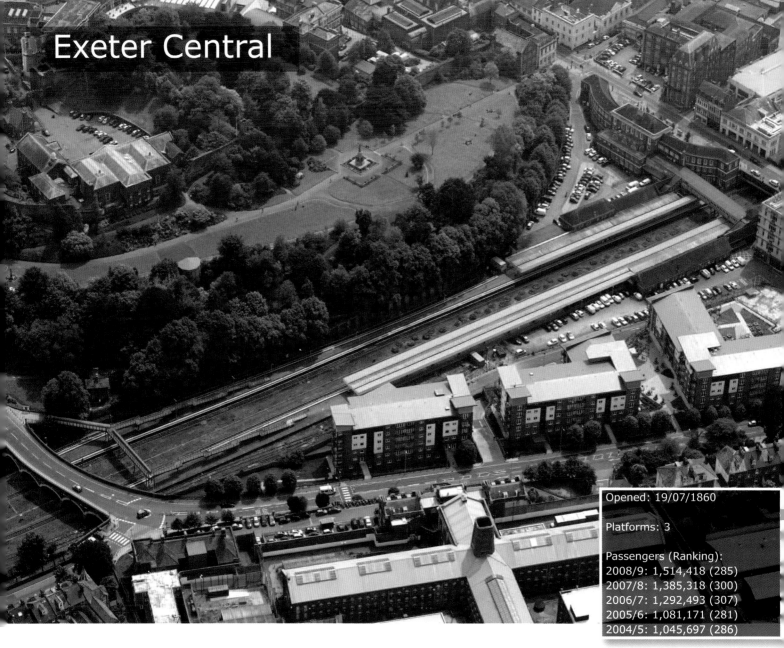

Opened: 19/07/1860

Platforms: 3

Passengers (Ranking):
2008/9: 1,514,418 (285)
2007/8: 1,385,318 (300)
2006/7: 1,292,493 (307)
2005/6: 1,081,171 (281)
2004/5: 1,045,697 (286)

Central station is Exeter's second railway station after St David's, but it is located right in the heart of the city centre meaning it still has considerable usage. The station was opened by the London & South Western Railway from Yeovil Junction, 16 years after St David's, and was originally known as Exeter Queen's Street. Other rail facilities built at the station included a 3 track loco shed and turntable to the east, just to the left of this photo, and there was also a goods shed to the north west. This is now the site of the three blocks of flats visible at the foot of the image at an angle to the main line, with the footprint of the triangular site still clearly visible. Central station is much the smaller of the two main stations, having only half the number of platforms, but is still used by an impressive amount of passengers, with over 1.5 million recorded in the last available figures. Following a fire in 1927 the station was rebuilt in 1931 to include four platforms, with two through lines running through the centre. It reopened on July 1st 1933 with an impressive curved entrance building, visible in the top right. It was with this reopening that the station was renamed to "Central". Today, the through lines remain, but there are now only three platforms in operation, including bay platform (on the far side) and two through platforms. The remain of the opposite bay can still be seen on the lower left, where there is still a section of decaying track in place. The awnings that covered thi platform are still also in place (middle right).

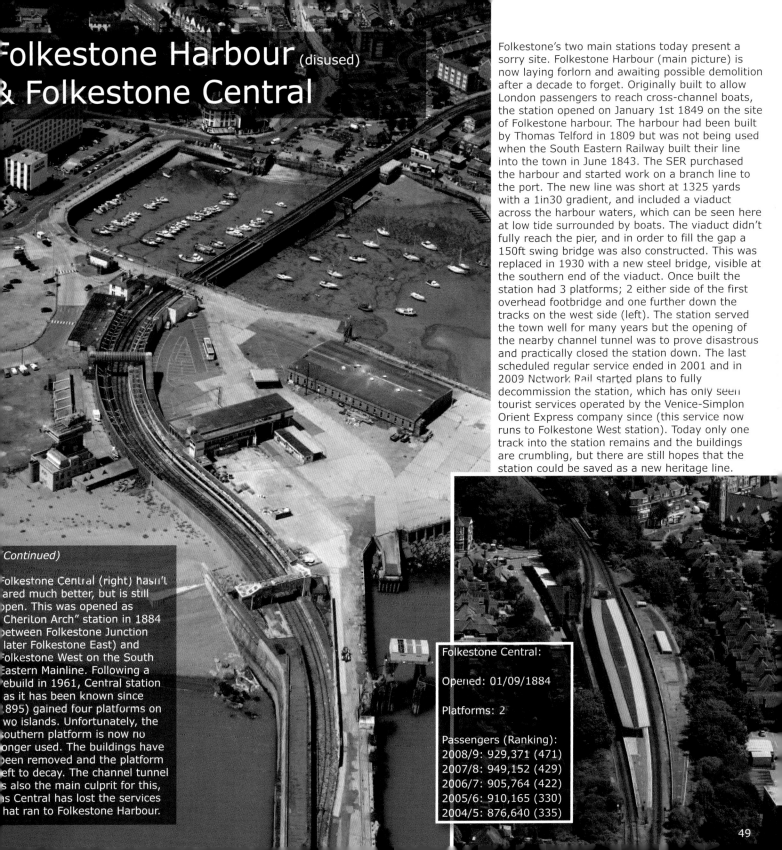

Folkestone Harbour (disused) & Folkestone Central

Folkestone's two main stations today present a sorry site. Folkestone Harbour (main picture) is now laying forlorn and awaiting possible demolition after a decade to forget. Originally built to allow London passengers to reach cross-channel boats, the station opened on January 1st 1849 on the site of Folkestone harbour. The harbour had been built by Thomas Telford in 1809 but was not being used when the South Eastern Railway built their line into the town in June 1843. The SER purchased the harbour and started work on a branch line to the port. The new line was short at 1325 yards with a 1in30 gradient, and included a viaduct across the harbour waters, which can be seen here at low tide surrounded by boats. The viaduct didn't fully reach the pier, and in order to fill the gap a 150ft swing bridge was also constructed. This was replaced in 1930 with a new steel bridge, visible at the southern end of the viaduct. Once built the station had 3 platforms; 2 either side of the first overhead footbridge and one further down the tracks on the west side (left). The station served the town well for many years but the opening of the nearby channel tunnel was to prove disastrous and practically closed the station down. The last scheduled regular service ended in 2001 and in 2009 Network Rail started plans to fully decommission the station, which has only seen tourist services operated by the Venice-Simplon Orient Express company since (this service now runs to Folkestone West station). Today only one track into the station remains and the buildings are crumbling, but there are still hopes that the station could be saved as a new heritage line.

(Continued)

Folkestone Central (right) hasn't fared much better, but is still open. This was opened as "Cheriton Arch" station in 1884 between Folkestone Junction (later Folkestone East) and Folkestone West on the South Eastern Mainline. Following a rebuild in 1961, Central station (as it has been known since 1895) gained four platforms on two islands. Unfortunately, the southern platform is now no longer used. The buildings have been removed and the platform left to decay. The channel tunnel is also the main culprit for this, as Central has lost the services that ran to Folkestone Harbour.

Folkestone Central:

Opened: 01/09/1884

Platforms: 2

Passengers (Ranking):
2008/9: 929,371 (471)
2007/8: 949,152 (429)
2006/7: 905,764 (422)
2005/6: 910,165 (330)
2004/5: 876,640 (335)

The Channel Tunnel

Situated on a site to the north west of Folkestone is the Channel Tunnel UK terminal, linking Britain with France and mainland Europe. Covering a site of 346 acres next to junction 12 of the M20, the "chunnel" whisks passengers under the English Channel to its sister station at Coquelles in only 35 minutes. Although plans had been mooted for almost two centuries for a tunnel, construction did not start until June 1988 on the modern scheme, with work commencing first on the French side. The UK side commenced work in December of that year, with both meeting in the middle two years later. When it opened in 1994 the land on this site had been transformed to include terminal buildings, freight lines, maintenance depots, and massive concrete "roll on" & "roll off" platforms designed for vehicles. The whole of the site stretched out for over 1½ miles. Despite its size the site was in fact quite constrained,

and its French equivalent covers a massive 1730 acres, dwarfing its U cousin. Because of this greater room, all of the rolling stock is based of the French side. The Eurostar trains have two decks designed for vehicles, allowing passengers to arrive directly from the motorway by car, drive onto the platforms, and depart for the other side. The massive platforms (opposite page) are around 864 yards long (2592ft There are currently 11 platforms on the UK side, but space has been left to take the number up to 16, if demand requires it.

Far Right, Opposite Page:
A Eurostar train makes its way through the Kent countryside.

Glasgow Central

The great Victorian city has perhaps one of the greatest Victorian stations. The Caledonian Railway's terminus is the final destination on the West Coast Main Line and is the busiest British station outside of London. Despite its importance, it was built relatively late compared to the city's other stations. The line into Glasgow originally only stretched to the south side of the River Clyde at Bridge Street station. Opened in August 1840 by the Glasgow & Paisley Joint Railway, the station building can just be seen to the left of the tracks at the very top of the image opposite. In the 1870s the Caledonian received permission to build a rail bridge over the Clyde and constructed an 8-platform station on the north bank of the river. This station forms the main part of the modern terminus, on the north side of Argyle Street. The station eventually featured a large ridge & furrow roof with a length of 560ft and a width of 213ft (the roof was a later addition, being built in 1882). The elegant booking hall and concourse were also added in 1882, followed a year later by the station's new Central Hotel on June 19th.

Both the hotel and the station were designed by the renowned Edinburgh architect Sir Robert Rowand Anderson. As the station's traffic began to increase a rebuild was required, which took place from 1899 to 1905. Designed this time by architect James Miller, the station was extended south over Argyle Street and the total number of platforms was increased to 13. Following the expansion, Bridge Street Station was to close, meaning all services from the south would now terminate at Central. Following remodelling in the last few years, the station now boast 15 platforms, with a new platform 13 due to open in 2010. It is also often referred to as the "High Level" station, due to the presence of a "Low Level" station below the main building, which opened in August 1896. This is in fact an entirely separate station built underground with two platforms at right angles to those in the main Central building. These platforms are now numbered 16 & 17 and are considered to be a part of the overall complex. This station is on the Argyle Line, which takes its name from the street above.

Glasgow Queen Street

Opened: 18/02/1842

Platforms: 7 (9 with Low Level)

Passengers (Ranking):
2008/9: 18,661,728 (16)
2007/8: 14,659,583 (20)
2006/7: 14,052,804 (20)
2005/6: 3,734,739 (64)
2004/5: 3,730,904 (64)

Like Central, Glasgow Queen Street features a "High Level" and "Low Level" station. The low level (opened in March 1886) also has two platforms at right angles to the main terminus building, taking the total number currently in operation to 9. From this angle, much of Queen Street today appears to be hidden from the air, being dwarfed by the bulk of the neighbouring Buchanan Galleries Shopping Centre (bottom right), but the platforms can just be made out under the road bridge. Opened by the Edinburgh & Glasgow Railway, the station is the terminus for the main services between the two cities, which run every 15 minutes. It is also the terminus for routes from northern Scotland. Nothing remains of the original station. It was rebuilt from 1878-1880 by James Carswell with a fine new iron-arched roof supported by iron Corinthian columns. The station is located just to the north of George Square near to Glasgow City Hall and today is the third busiest in Scotland and one of the busiest in the UK. Since 2006/7 the number of passengers using the station has rocketed, straining the already crowded capacity on the approach to the station through the Queen Street Tunnel. There are plans to expand the platforms to enable longer carriages to be able to use the station, but work on the scheme has yet to reach the construction stage. At one point the station did have 9 above ground platforms, and new ones may only be the answer to the overcrowding problems that Queen Street is currently facing.

Glasgow St Enoch (site of)

Opened: 01/05/1876

Closed: 27/06/1966

Platforms: 12

St Enoch's sad demise is perhaps the greatest of any station to be closed as a consequence of the Beeching cuts. St Enoch was a huge station and covered an area almost as large as the rebuilt Glasgow Central Station. St Enoch was located just over 100 yards to the east of Glasgow Central, but was at a right angle and faced westwards. Despite this, the approach to the station was much the same, coming across the River Clyde from the south before making a sharp left turn. It was opened by the City of Glasgow Union Railway in 1876 and featured 6 platforms covered by an imposing barrelled roof. The roof was an impressive 525 feet in length, as well as 205ft wide and 83ft high. Perhaps its most impressive feature, however, was the St Enoch Hotel at the entrance to the building, which faced out onto St Enoch Square (top Left). This was a classic Victorian railway hotel and had six storeys, with 200 rooms amongst its facilities. The station was rebuilt from 1898-1902 by the Glasgow & South Western Railway, who had taken over the CGUR in 1883. Six more platforms were added under a slightly smaller roof that was built alongside the original. This second roof measured 293 feet 7 inches in length, by 143ft wide and 65ft high. The site of the station today is home to the St Enoch Centre, a major shopping centre that was opened in May 1989. Following closure, the station buildings had remained standing until 1977 before they were demolished, along with the hotel. The land then acted as a car park until work started on the shopping centre in 1986. The viaduct that carried the line into the station is still standing, but now lies unused, while the rest of the land occupied by the long platforms is now used as a car park.

Glasgow Depots

Glasgow Corkerhill T.M.D.

Now located next to the M77, there has been a depot on this site since December 1st 1896. Opened by the Glasgow & South Western Railway, the original Corkerhill was an extremely rural location at the time of opening, and took its name from the adjacent Corkerhill Farm. Built on the Paisley Canal Station line to relieve overcrowded sheds at St Enoch Station, the site featured an engine shed and turntable to the north east, as well as a large number of sidings. Now the site services diesel units and has recently been extended with new maintenance and washing sheds.

Glasgow Polmadie T.C.C.

Polmadie Train Care Centre, as it is now known, was built by the Caledonian Railway around 1879 on the route into the centre of Glasgow and the new Central Station. It is a familiar feature for many passengers, as all West Coast Main Line services pass the depot on their way in or out of the city. It primarily services the Virgin Pendolino trains that use the WCML routes, and for much of its life was referred t as Polmadie CARMD (Carriage Maintenance Depot). The original depot featured a large brick shed with 14 tracks and had seven through roads. There was also a turntable and a mineral depot, where the mineral coal wagons would have been serviced.

Halifax

Opened: 01/07/1844

Platforms: 2

Passengers (Ranking):
2008/9: 1,469,932 (299)
2007/8: 1,098,836 (384)
2006/7: 1,049,085 (380)
2005/6:   978,225 (312)
2004/5:   940,437 (316)

Whilst it is still a perfectly functional station, Halifax Station has certainly seen better days in its history. At one point there were 7 platforms and associated works, sidings (on the site of the car park) and engine sheds (towards the top right), but today there are now just 2 platforms, and the old main entrance building is no longer part of the station. Built by the Manchester & Leeds Railway, the original station was called Shaw Syke and located just a few hundred yards to the west. The line was extended through the current site in August 1850, and the new station built on the existing site. The impressive station building (inset), built in honey-coloured limestone, was opened in 1855 to a design by Thomas Butterworth. It is now Grade II listed and forms part of the adjacent "Eureka" children's museum site (right). In the mid 1870s the Great Northern Railway built a new line through the station that would see it extended to 6 through platforms and a tiny bay platform at the southern end, next to the station building. Its remains are hidden by the line of trees immediately to the right of the main building in the smaller photograph. A new island platform was added in front of the station building with the redevelopment, but this no longer stands. In 1890 the station was renamed "Halifax Old Station" to distinguish it from Halifax St Paul's and Halifax North Bridge. It was renamed again to "Halifax Town" in 1951, but reverted to just "Halifax" ten years later.

Harrogate

Opened: 01/08/1862

Platforms: 3

Passengers (Ranking):
2008/9: 1,204,486 (357)
2007/8: 1,180,509 (356)
2006/7: 1,141,712 (342)
2005/6: 1,096,944 (273)
2004/5: 1,054,919 (283)

When the railway came to elegant Harrogate the town was still a small village in North Yorkshire, famed for its spring waters and peaceful air. Its arrival would enable the town to grow and allow more visitors the opportunity to enjoy its famous baths, but this wasn't without concern. At the time there was disharmony amongst some locals as it was believed that the coming of the railway coming could precipitate the arrival of the "Proles" and spoil its genteel character. Today, as well as being a tourist destination, the city is an important commuter link between York and Leeds. Built by the North Eastern Railway, nothing of the old station remains today, following a rebuild around 1965 that has resulted in a utilitarian station distinctly lacking in character. There are 3 platforms, including a small north-facing bay platform (No. 2). Whilst the railway's presence was small in the growing town, 200 yards further north there was a small depot and goods shed near Bower Road. This is now the site of a supermarket. The station site now forms part of a modern interchange, with an adjoining bus station.

Hastings

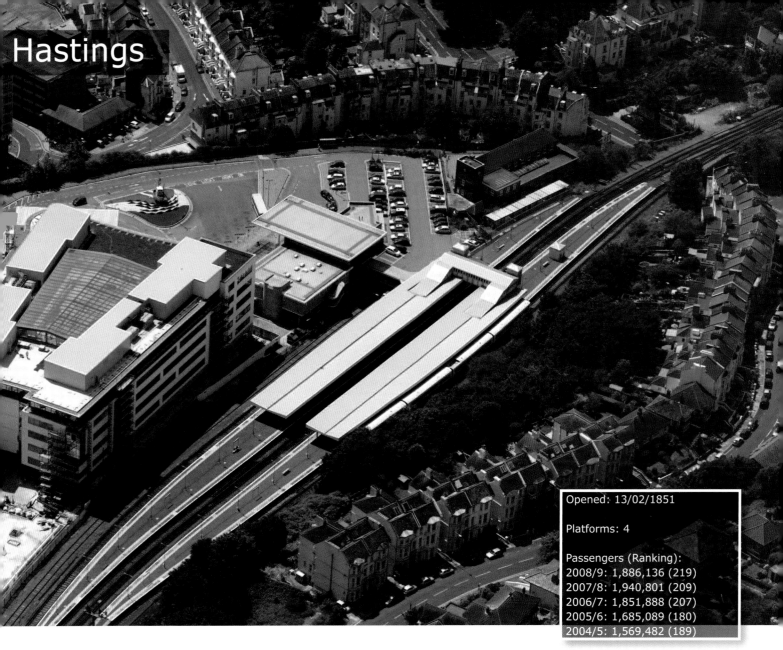

Opened: 13/02/1851

Platforms: 4

Passengers (Ranking):
2008/9: 1,886,136 (219)
2007/8: 1,940,801 (209)
2006/7: 1,851,888 (207)
2005/6: 1,685,089 (180)
2004/5: 1,569,482 (189)

¹hat looks to be a perfectly functional, small station, actually has a scinating history of competition by competing railway companies. The righton, Lewes & Hastings Railway was the first company permitted to ild a route into the town in 1844, which would terminate at ilverhythe, now a modern suburb in the west of Hastings. This line as granted permission to be extended to Ashford in 1845, but after ie BL&HR were taken over by the London & Brighton Railway, the outh Eastern Railway objected to the new line. They put forward their wn route, but ended up being given the rights to the Ashford line. The &BR was subsequently to become the London, Brighton & South Coast ailway, and they had retained a one mile stretch of land on the new ute, meaning that they would be free to use the new SER line and ations without charge. Subsequently, the station at Hastings was

actually two stations in a v
shape; one was a through station for the SER, and the second was a terminus for the LB&SCR. The terminus station was situated behind the curved row of houses at the top of the picture, and followed the route of the road. The entire station complex was completely rebuilt by the Southern Railway in 1931 to the layout that exists today. It opened on July 5th with two new island platforms and very little trace of the old terminus. The station received a £7million overhaul in 2003 with a new entrance and booking hall, which opened in October 2004. The site of a former goods shed on the left is being redeveloped as part of the £71million mixed use "Station Plaza" project, the first building of which is a new campus for the Sussex Coast College, next to the station entrance block.

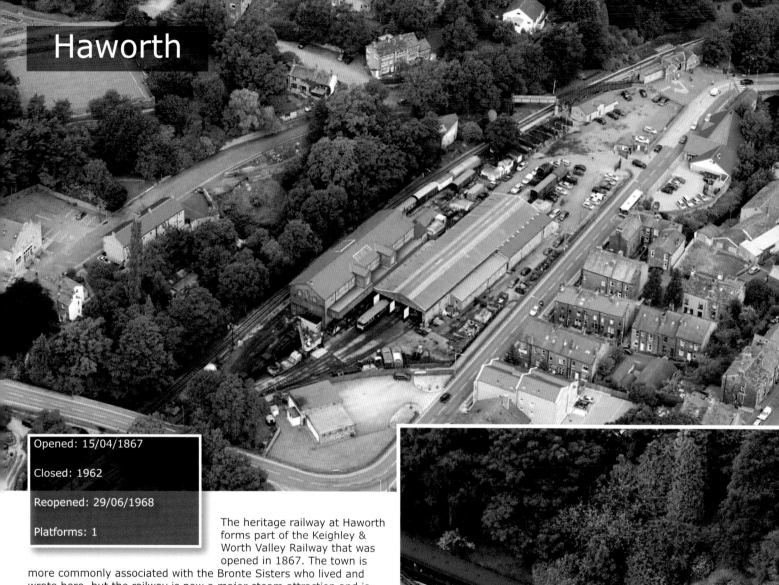

Haworth

Opened: 15/04/1867

Closed: 1962

Reopened: 29/06/1968

Platforms: 1

The heritage railway at Haworth forms part of the Keighley & Worth Valley Railway that was opened in 1867. The town is more commonly associated with the Bronte Sisters who lived and wrote here, but the railway is now a major steam attraction and is the headquarters of the preserved line. Unlike most railways, the line was built by local factory owners who were intent on providing their mills with regular supplies of coal. The running of the trains was actually leased out to the Midland Railway, and they would eventually purchase the line in 1892 after long held interest from the Great Northern Railway, the Midland's main rivals in the area.

The Midland extended the station building at Haworth but did not extend the track. There is only one track along most of the route, although room was left for a second when it was first constructed with space being left beneath the route's bridges. The line remained open until it was forced to close in 1962. A group of locals and railway enthusiasts then set up a society with the aim of preserving the original line, and it was to reopen on June 29th 1968. The site at Haworth also holds the main locomotive works and engine shed on the K&WVR, where works on the steam engines, diesel locomotives and diesel multiple units takes place.

Holyhead

Opened: September 1851

Platforms: 3

Passengers (Ranking):
2008/9: 184,628 (1278)
2007/8: 209,053 (1125)
2006/7: 212,266 (1077)
2005/6: 202.033 (1042)
2004/5: 215,184 (978)

yhead has long been the primary seaport to Ireland for centuries, d this history is intertwined with the railways, and more specifically Irish Mail. The mail service between London and Dublin gained ater importance with the 1800 Act of Union between Great Britain d Ireland, meaning that the Irish Mail needed to be delivered as ckly as possible. The route through Holyhead to the mail boats was quickest until the railways came to Liverpool, meaning a much rtened journey time could be achieved. From 1839 the route though erpool was used instead, hastening the need for a north Wales coast e to Anglesey. The Chester & Holyhead Railway was consequently set in July 1844 to build the line. It reached Holyhead in August 1st 18 with a temporary terminus. A new extension was to be built to niralty Pier that opened on May 20th 1851 with a new permanent tion following in September 1851. The London & North Western took er the C&HR in 1858, and they developed the site around the station

with new platforms and a goods shed around 1870. The station site was rebuilt again in 1880 to better meet the requirements for the large number of passengers, opening for service on June 17th. There were 4 platforms built in a v shape either side of the dock and an impressive 65-bed hotel built between them. A clock tower built to mark the opening of the station by the Prince of Wales was sited in the rear courtyard of the building. The hotel was demolished in 1951 and there is now an office block on the site. The clock, however, has been repositioned in front of it (bottom left). Today, the station has 3 platforms - the track to the fourth in the covered shed (on the right) has been lifted – and it also retains some of the original sidings (middle left). These used to stretch further along the side of the dock to the very top right.

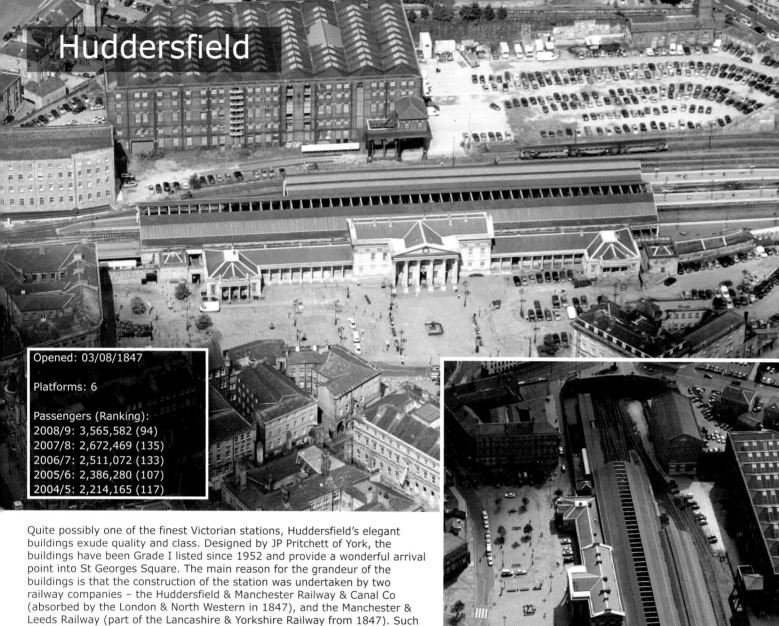

Huddersfield

Opened: 03/08/1847

Platforms: 6

Passengers (Ranking):
2008/9: 3,565,582 (94)
2007/8: 2,672,469 (135)
2006/7: 2,511,072 (133)
2005/6: 2,386,280 (107)
2004/5: 2,214,165 (117)

Quite possibly one of the finest Victorian stations, Huddersfield's elegant buildings exude quality and class. Designed by JP Pritchett of York, the buildings have been Grade I listed since 1952 and provide a wonderful arrival point into St Georges Square. The main reason for the grandeur of the buildings is that the construction of the station was undertaken by two railway companies – the Huddersfield & Manchester Railway & Canal Co (absorbed by the London & North Western in 1847), and the Manchester & Leeds Railway (part of the Lancashire & Yorkshire Railway from 1847). Such was the enthusiasm for the new station that when the foundation stone was laid on October 9th 1846 a public holiday was declared in celebration. The station partly opened in 1847 with a single platform, but was not completed until October 1850. The main building in the centre is flanked by two identical wings with single storey buildings. These were the original booking offices for the two railway companies. They have since been converted into pubs that are accessible from the main platforms. On the left is "The Head of Steam" (the former LNWR office), and on the right "The King's Head" (L&Y). For many years this pub was known as "The Station Tavern". Also of note is the large 1883 St George's goods warehouse in the background. At the front of the station is a goods lift, and the site of the track that served it can still be seen below. This building is now Grade II listed and has recently been redeveloped at a cost of £21.5million into an office complex, after laying empty for nearly 3 decades.

Hull

Opened: 08/05/1848

Platforms: 11 (7 in use)

Passengers (Ranking):
2008/9: 2,162,500 (190)
2007/8: 2,112,980 (188)
2006/7: 2,050,545 (175)
2005/6: 1,969,919 (145)
2004/5: 1,961,298 (139)

Known for many years as "Hull Paragon", the station has recently undergone a major upgrade as part of the construction of a new £18m transport interchange now called "Hull Paragon Interchange". Opened on September 16th 2007, the new interchange at the front of the building makes use of some of the classic Victorian features of this fine station. The original, built by the York & North Midland Railway, was much smaller, comprising of a 3-bay pitched roof train shed and a superb entrance and booking hall with Italianate façade and porte-cochere on the south side (right). A railway hotel was built along with the station, opening in 1849. Queen Victoria was among the quests here in 1854, resulting in it being renamed the "Royal Station Hotel". The station was considerably enlarged in 1905 when a new 5-bay glass and iron roof was added along with more platforms. The hotel was also extended at this time, but it had to be rebuilt following a fire in 1990. Both structures have been Grade II* listed since October 1952. Today, although Hull station still has 11 platforms only seven are in use. The bays on the north side of the main shed are no longer used, and now act as car parking (centre). The open-air platforms on the south side (right centre) are dilapidated and unused. These were the platforms used by many eastern Europeans who were fleeing Russian outbreaks of anti-Semitism in the late 19th century. They used Hull as a port of call on their voyages to a new life in the USA. Since this image was taken the open land next to the station has been redeveloped as St Stephen's Shopping Centre.

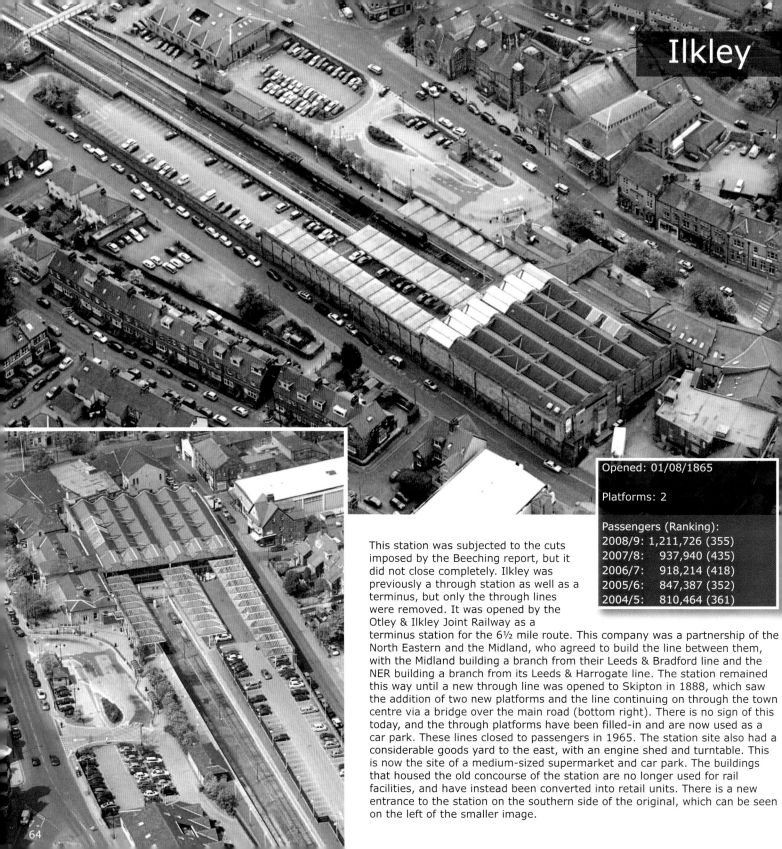

Ilkley

Opened: 01/08/1865

Platforms: 2

Passengers (Ranking):
2008/9: 1,211,726 (355)
2007/8:   937,940 (435)
2006/7:   918,214 (418)
2005/6:   847,387 (352)
2004/5:   810,464 (361)

This station was subjected to the cuts imposed by the Beeching report, but it did not close completely. Ilkley was previously a through station as well as a terminus, but only the through lines were removed. It was opened by the Otley & Ilkley Joint Railway as a terminus station for the 6½ mile route. This company was a partnership of the North Eastern and the Midland, who agreed to build the line between them, with the Midland building a branch from their Leeds & Bradford line and the NER building a branch from its Leeds & Harrogate line. The station remained this way until a new through line was opened to Skipton in 1888, which saw the addition of two new platforms and the line continuing on through the town centre via a bridge over the main road (bottom right). There is no sign of this today, and the through platforms have been filled-in and are now used as a car park. These lines closed to passengers in 1965. The station site also had a considerable goods yard to the east, with an engine shed and turntable. This is now the site of a medium-sized supermarket and car park. The buildings that housed the old concourse of the station are no longer used for rail facilities, and have instead been converted into retail units. There is a new entrance to the station on the southern side of the original, which can be seen on the left of the smaller image.

Ipswich

Opened: 01/07/1860

Platforms: 4

Passengers (Ranking):
2008/9: 2,825,352 (128)
2007/8: 2,807,395 (122)
2006/7: 2,402,052 (142)
2005/6: 2,144,935 (125)
2004/5: 2,017,300 (130)

Ipswich station is situated by the banks of the River Orwell to the south of the town centre. It was not the first station in the town, but is close to the location of the original terminus built by the Eastern Union Railway in 1846. This station was south east of the present site, on the opposite side of the Ipswich Tunnel, near what is now Station Street. Here there was also a large locomotive depot and associated sidings. The tunnel was constructed by the EUR to link the town with Ely. At 361 yards long it is the only tunnel on the Great Eastern Line, the route that links Norwich with London Liverpool Street Station, via Ipswich. The station was replaced by the existing facility in 1860 after the old one was deemed to be inadequate for trains coming from the north, which had to reverse into the station. The station was extended by the Great Eastern Railway in 1880 with the addition of a new island platform. It has always been well placed to service the freight traffic that uses the nearby port at Felixstowe, and the sidings at the station are still used for stabling the freight locomotives. Recently the old loco depot site has been redeveloped for housing, with the streets named after the engineers who were responsible for building the railway infrastructure in the town.

Isle Of White Steam Railway

The Isle of White Steam Railway is one of the best-preserved heritage railways in the country. It has its headquarters at Havenstreet Station (above) on the line between Wootton and Smallbrook, a distance of just over 5 miles. The railway's main engine shed and carriage and wagon workshop are located here, along with a museum and refreshment room. The railway was initially built as part of the Isle of White Central Railway from Ryde to Newport in 1875, starting at Smallbrook Junction. It opened on December 20th and would last until the all services were closed on February 21st 1966. Havenstreet station opened with the railway in 1875, later changing its name from "Haven Street" (the name of the village) in 1958. Today it is the largest station on the restored line with other visitor attractions built around it.

The Isle of White Steam Railway was founded on January 24th 1971 b a small group of enthusiasts who had formed the "Isle of White Railwa Company" to preserve the line in all of its glory. Today the line has on of the best and most varied collections of rolling stock of any heritage railway in Britain, thanks in part to the Isle of White's railways having to use second hand engines from the mainland for most of its history. is planning to expand further, with the aim of reopening other parts o the original line at some point in the future, including the line back int Ryde.

Keighley

Opened: 06/03/1847

Platforms: 4
(2 National Rail, 2 K&WVR)

Passengers (Ranking):
2008/9: 1,492,776 (295)
2007/8: 1,182,704 (354)
2006/7: 1,155,471 (337)
2005/6: 1,127,154 (270)
2004/5: 1,087,690 (274)

he site at Keighley was the location for a huge number of railway elated works, with dozens of factories, both small and huge, based ght next to the station. To the south there was a major Great orthern depot and shed (just off the bottom left of the image), and to he north west there was an equally large Midland depot (just off the op centre). The station was opened as a major stop on the Leeds & radford Extension Railway running from Shipley to Colne. This was an xtension of the Leeds & Bradford Railway, and was actually started hilst the Leeds to Bradford line was under construction. The Midland ook over the running of the new company in July 1846, well before eighley Station was completed in 1847, and was finally absorbed in uly 1851. The original station was built to the north of the bridge in

the photograph, but was rebuilt in May 1883 on the southern side. The station today is still open for mainline services, but is also the terminus for the Keighley & Worth Valley Railway (see Haworth). After Keighley, the line runs to Ingrow (West), Damems (the smallest station in Britain, with a platform one carriage length long), Oakworth (where the 1970 film "the Railway Children" was shot), Haworth and Oxenhope. The modern station is owned by Network rail, but the K&WVR rents platforms 3 & 4 (on the left), whilst Northern Rail rents 1 & 2 (on the right) for mainline services. Of note in the image is the preserved turntable, which has been relocated from Hawes Junction (now Garsdale) in Cumbria.

Kettering

Opened: May 1857

Platforms: 4

Passengers (Ranking):
2008/9: 1,112,390 (399)
2007/8: 1,085,989 (387)
2006/7: 1,012,009 (384)
2005/6:   920,850 (323)
2004/5:   933,270 (319)

Kettering is a fine example of an original Midland Railway station, with impressive original features including ornate iron awnings and pillars, along with glazed ridge and furrow platform roofs. Designed by Charles Henry Driver, the station took a long time to reach fruition. In 1847 the Midland Railway was granted permission to build an extension line from the Great Northern Railway at Hitchin to Northampton and Huntingdon. Despite this, a new Act of Parliament was required in 1848, which was presented with a petition from the people of Kettering explaining why a railway would be good for the town. One of the main benefits was described as the ability to export shipments of coal more cheaply, as several deposits had been found in the area at the time. The line and the station finally opened a full ten years after permission was first granted. On that day in 1857, a town holiday was declared, and excursions were held on the first trains to Southill Park in Bedfordshire.

The station was extended in the late 19th century by the famous Midland architect Charles Trubshaw, who designed the main entrance building. Along with the station there was also a sizable engine shed to the north on the site of the station car park, with the approach tracks coming in from the northern side in the top left of the photograph. The shape of the sidings and shed is still extremely noticeable in the shape of the car park. The end of the shed reached the very edge of the main entrance road leading into the station, which can be seen heading away towards the top right of the picture. The ornate iron platform roofs were threatened with demolition by British Rail in the early 1970s due to the cost of maintaining them. However, following protests from the Kettering Civic Society, they were saved and eventually restored, ensuring the station retained its splendid character.

Kidderminster

Like something out of a bygone age, Kidderminster has two separate railway stations, operated by two separate companies, right next to each other. These are the national rail Kidderminster Station (top centre, under the road bridge) and the heritage line Kidderminster Town Station (top left) on the Severn Valley Railway.

Kidderminster Station was originally built on the Worcester to Stourbridge line, which was built by the Oxford, Worcester & Wolverhampton Railway in 1852. Originally the station had a mock-Tudor entrance hall, but this was replaced around 1968 with a more utilitarian building that still stands. The station is still an important link to Birmingham and the rest of the West Midlands, but it is certainly overshadowed in style by its more recent neighbour.

Situated on the site of the old station goods yard, the remainder of which is now a shared car park, Kidderminster Town is the southern terminus for the Severn Valley Railway from Bridgnorth. Originally starting at Hartlebury, the SVR was extended to Kidderminster in 1878. The Victorian style station features 3 platforms, a museum and a refreshment room, and opened on July 30th 1984.

At the foot of the image can be seen a large shed. This is a carriage store, cleaning works and maintenance shed for the SVR that opened in 2003. Also of note is some of the rolling stock and the turntable in the yard between the shed and the station, next to Kidderminster Harriers FC's stadium.

Opened: 01/05/1852

Platforms: 2

Passengers (Ranking):
2008/9: 1,227,492 (351)
2007/8:   963,041 (420)
2006/7:   866,145 (438)
2005/6:   805,496 (370)
2004/5:   734,132 (397)

Leeds City Station is an amalgamation of two former stations, Wellington Station and Leeds New Station, which were combined in 1938. Most of the modern station is based on the site of the old New Station. The first of the two to be built was Wellington Station, which was constructed by the Leeds and Bradford Railway in 1846. Only part of the station site was incorporated into City Station in 1938, but its outline can still be seen today. The first two arches of the modern station roof are part of the site of Wellington Station, as are the adjacent car parks next to the River Aire (below). Leeds New Station was built from 1866-9 by the North Eastern Railway Company and the London & North Western Railway. Its construction necessitated the building of a viaduct from Marsh Lane over Briggate to link the station with the Leeds and Selby Railway line to the east (top right, opposite), which had been constructed in 1834. This allowed through traffic to pass through Leeds city centre. To the south of the site, New Station was built over a series of arches spanning the River Aire, now known as The Dark Arches (bottom). The station effectively acted as a roof over the arches, creating a covered street. Originally these arches were used for storage, but now contain shops and restaurants. In 1967 the station was completely rebuilt and a new metal roof built overhead. Between 1999 and 2002 it underwent a further major rebuilding at a cost of £245 million. The station was expanded from 12 to 17 platforms, with new platforms on the south side and additional approach tracks at the western end. The metal roof added in 1967 was removed and replaced with a new structure that allows in more light. The number of passengers using the station increased significantly during the last year of available records (2008/9). This could help bring forward plans for the construction of new platforms on the remainder of the old Wellington Station site, which is currently a car park, as capacity could soon be reached. Today, Leeds City Station is the largest in England outside of London with a total of 17 platforms, including 11 bay and 6 through platforms.

Leeds City
& Leeds Central (site of)

The old Leeds Central Station on Wellington Street (right) was opened in 1854 and was a joint project by the Manchester and Leeds Railway and the London and North Western Railway. The station closed in 1967 when all services were moved to the new City Station. The site was used for a Royal Mail sorting office and later became a retail park, with only the viaduct over the river and an old hydraulic wagon lift (centre) remaining. The lift is a Grade II listed building and was one of three towers used to move wagons from the high level Lancashire & Yorkshire Railway sidings to the lower level Great Northern Railway goods yard. The site is now being redeveloped at a cost of £300 million as the mixed use "Wellington Place" development, where the lift will become the centrepiece of a new public square.

Until 1969 this station was known as "Leicester London Road" to distinguish it from Leicester Central (1899-1969), which was on the other side of town. The original station had a single 165 yard long platform with the booking hall and entrance buildings on the west side. It was entered via Campbell Street (far right, bottom image). Much of the site and approach road is now occupied by the large car park.

London Road station was built by the Midland Counties Railway (later a part of the Midland Railway) and designed by William Parsons. The station would later acquire a second platform in 1858, which was then turned into an island platform a decade later. The present layout was adopted in the late 19th century when the Midland Railway decided to rebuild the site, comprising of two new island platforms on the site of the originals, as well as a fine new entrance and booking hall designed by Charles Trubshaw.

The rebuilt station was completed by 1894, and also included a large porte-cochere facing the main road. The vehicular entrances to the porte-cochere can be seen in the station façade in the top photo.

Further north west there was a large maintenance depot about 200 yards further along the tracks. Separate sheds for both the Midland and the London & North Western Railway were located here on the western side of the tracks. There was also a large roundhouse on the eastern side that opened around 1952, replacing two smaller roundhouses.

Leicester

Opened: 04/05/1840

Platforms: 4

Passengers (Ranking):
2008/9: 5,132,022 (58)
2007/8: 4,969,109 (60)
2006/7: 4,778,063 (63)
2005/6: 4,360,891 (52)
2004/5: 4,456,662 (51)

Liverpool Crown Street (site of)

This is the site of the western terminus of the world's first inter-city passenger railway. The Liverpool & Manchester Railway was opened on September 13th 1830 between Liverpool Crown Street and Manchester Liverpool Road. Built to enable cotton from the mills in Manchester to reach the port at Liverpool (and raw materials to go in the other direction) the railway proved so popular that the station here would only last for six years before it was replaced by a much larger one at Liverpool Lime Street. Crown Street closed on August 15th 1836. Carriages into the station entered via a single-track tunnel from Edge Hill station to the east. Running 291 yards, it was designed by George Stephenson. The carriages were pulled up into the station by a cable and returned to Edge Hill under the force of gravity, because the locomotives could not enter the tunnel due to the gradient being too

steep for them to handle. A second, much larger tunnel was constructed under the station around 1830, running parallel with the original. Known as the Wapping Tunnel, this connected Edge Hill to the Liverpool Docks and ran for around 2250 yards. The chimney visible on the left is one of three surviving ventilation shafts for the Wapping Tunnel. A third parallel tunnel was to open in 1846. The entrance to this tunnel can be seen in the top right corner. By this time Crown Street had been converted into a goods yard that would last until 1972. The whole yard was landscaped in the 1980s and is now a public park, although the small section of track visible in the cuttings is still used for occasional shunting for freight trains using Edge Hill. Wapping Tunnel and the 1830 Crown Street tunnel remain buried under the site.

Liverpool Lime Street

Opened: 15/08/1836

Platforms: 9

Passengers (Ranking):
2008/9: 10,833,012 (29)
2007/8:   4,338,760 (69)
2006/7:   6,377,363 (40)
2005/6: 14,472,431 (17)
2004/5: 13,535,200 (17)

ime Street is the largest station of any kind in Liverpool, but
urprisingly it is no longer the busiest. That honour now belongs to
iverpool Central, which is on the underground section of the Merseyrail
etwork. In 2008/09 a total of 19,635,814 people used the three-
latform station, far exceeding the numbers at Lime Street, which also
as a single-platform underground station on the city-centre loop. The
and on which the station sits was the original site of the cattle market,
nd was purchased from the council for £9,000 by the Manchester &
iverpool Railway. Lime Street was built from 1833-1836 to replace
rown Street Station, but like its counterpart it first had to use cables to
ull passenger coaches into the terminus from Edge Hill (and use
ravity on the way out) until locomotives became sufficiently powerful
o handle the ascent and descent. The station was rebuilt in 1849 by Sir
Villiam Tite, this time on a slightly different footing a few yards to the

north, running parallel to Lord Nelson Street. The new building featured
the world's first iron-segmental arch vaulted roof. The rear wall that
supported this roof is still extant in the current station, and is next to
platform one. The London & North Western had taken control of the
station by 1867 when the next major rebuild started. This included a
brand new glass and iron roof with a span of 219ft designed by William
Baker. This is the north barrel of the existing roof (top). The south shed,
by Francis Stevenson and EW Ives, was added in 1874, spanning a
further 186ft. The magnificent building at the front of the station is the
1871 Great North Western Hotel by Alfred Waterhouse. Since 1997 this
building has housed student flats for the nearby John Moores University.
Both the hotel and the station are Grade II listed. The hotel has been
listed since June 1952, and the station since March 1975.

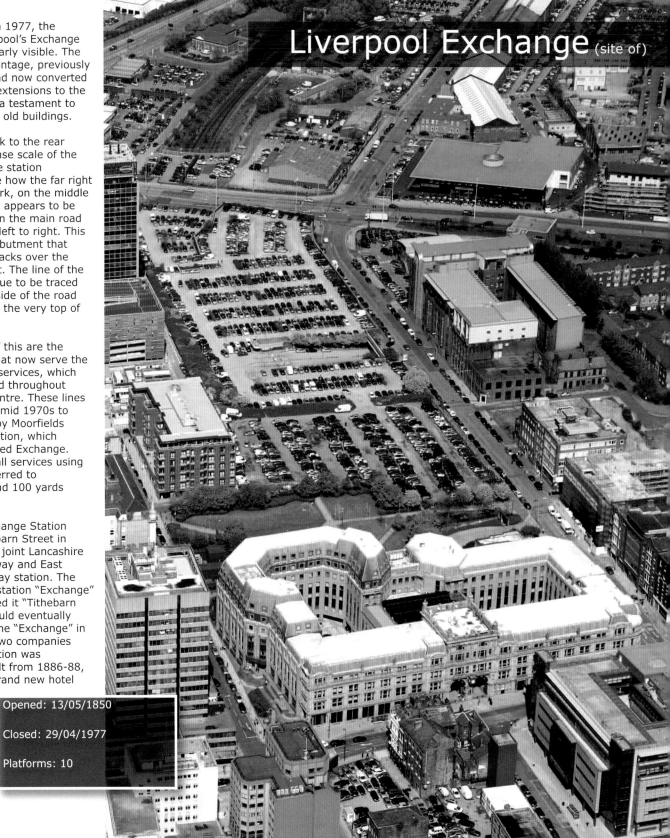

Despite closing in 1977, the footprint of Liverpool's Exchange Station is still clearly visible. The ornate station frontage, previously a station hotel and now converted into offices with extensions to the rear, survives as a testament to the quality of the old buildings.

The large car park to the rear shows the immense scale of the platforms and the station approaches. Note how the far right of the end car park, on the middle left of the image, appears to be raised higher than the main road which runs from left to right. This was part of the abutment that carried the rail tracks over the road on a viaduct. The line of the tracks can continue to be traced on the opposite side of the road (Leeds Street) to the very top of the image.

Just to the left of this are the existing tracks that now serve the city's Merseyrail services, which runs underground throughout Liverpool City Centre. These lines were built in the mid 1970s to service the nearby Moorfields Underground Station, which effectively replaced Exchange. When it closed, all services using Exchange transferred to Moorfields, around 100 yards further south.

The original Exchange Station opened as Tithebarn Street in 1850, and was a joint Lancashire & Yorkshire Railway and East Lancashire Railway station. The L&YR called the station "Exchange" and the ELR called it "Tithebarn Street". They would eventually settle on the name "Exchange" in 1859 when the two companies merged. The station was completely rebuilt from 1886-88, when it got its grand new hotel and ten long platforms.

Liverpool Exchange (site of)

Opened: 13/05/1850

Closed: 29/04/1977

Platforms: 10

Liverpool South Parkway

Opened: 11/06/2006

Platforms: 6

Passengers (Ranking):
2008/9: 568,822 (674)
2007/8: 419,681 (755)
2006/7: 288,845 (918)
2005/6: n/a
2004/5: n/a

One of the newest and most striking stations in the country is situated in the south of Liverpool, between the areas of Garston and Allerton. Costing a total of £32 million, Liverpool South Parkway Station is designed to be a modern interchange, linking road, rail and bus with facilities for bicycles and taxis. The station also links 3 different rail lines and has been designed to improve transport connections to the nearby Liverpool John Lennon Airport. On the left are the Merseyrail Northern Lines that eventually reach Southport, and on the right are the National Rail lines that include the West Coast Main Line and the Manchester line via Warrington. These 4 platforms are built on the site of Allerton Station, which was demolished in 2005 to make way for the development of South Parkway. The station also features a bus interchange and a large concourse behind a curved 30ft glazed outer wall (on the far side of the picture), and it has been designed to be an eco-friendly building. The roof was built using 2.3 tonnes of recycled aluminium and the station also features energy-generating solar panels amongst its attributes. Originally, the estimate for the cost was about half of the final total and the station ended up opening almost six months later than planned. Nevertheless, passenger numbers have increased steadily in the few years since it has opened.

Llangollen

The Llangollen Railway runs along the banks of the River Dee in some of the most stunning countryside in north Wales. Running for 7½ miles from Llangollen to Carrog, the railway is now a well-preserved heritage line open for steam tourists.

It was formed in 1975 by a group of steam enthusiasts from the remnants of the Great Western Railway's Ruabon to Barmouth line that opened between 1862 and 1867. The part of the route from here at Llangollen to Corwen was opened on May 1st 1850. The line closed, like so many, on January 18th 1965 due to the cuts implemented by the Beeching Report. It remained open for goods traffic until 1968, before closing completely. Most of the tracks and signalling was removed, but a few stations retained their buildings, including Llangollen and Carrog.

The Flint and Deeside Railway Preservation Society was set up in 1972 with a view to preserving one of the standard gauge lines in the north of Wales. When the line around Llangollen became available in 1975 they secured a lease from the local council, who had acquired the line after closure. Work started on restoring the route on July 1st that year. By September 13th sufficient length of track had been put down (about 60ft) for the first new steam trip to take place and for the society to hold an open day in celebration.

The site at Llangollen is also home to the railway's main locomotive and maintenance shed (right), which is the original GWR shed and is Grade II listed. In the future it is hoped that the line can be extended still further by the reopening of the 2½ mile section to Corwen Town, which would involve the building of a new station. Planning permission for the new line was sought in April 2010, and was granted in late August 2010 by the Welsh Assembly.

London Blackfriars

Opened: 10/05/1886

Platforms: 5

Passengers (Ranking):
2008/9: 12,959,108 (25)
2007/8: 12,440,374 (25)
2006/7: 11,852,397 (24)
2005/6: 8,258,915 (25)
2004/5: 7,782,674 (25)

This is an image that already looks completely out of date, as Blackfriars Station is currently undergoing a massive £350million redevelopment as part of the Thameslink programme. Once finished, the new station will feature platforms that span the entire length of the river Thames – the first station in London to do so. There will also be a new southern station with entrances on the south bank of the river, whilst the entire length of the bridge will be covered with a new glazed roof. The buildings at the north bank will be rebuilt with a new concourse providing better links to Blackfriars Underground Station, which will also be enhanced as part of the development. Work started in March 22nd 2009 when the three bay platforms (on the right hand side) were closed. The new station is expected to be fully completed by mid 2012, and will allow much longer 12-car trains to pass through the line. The station originally opened in 1886 as St Paul's on the London, Chatham & Dover Railway. At the time there was already an

Underground station on the site, which had commenced services on May 30th 1870. A new bridge was constructed with the mainline station and named St Paul's Railway Bridge. It was built next to an existing bridge that dated from 1864, known as Blackfriars Railway Bridge. This bridge carried the railway over the Thames from the now defunct Blackfriars Bridge Station (1864-1964) on the south bank of the river. By the mid 1980s the bridge was deemed to be too weak to carry modern trains, and it was dismantled in 1985. The red columns reaching out of the river on the west side of the new station bridge (left) are all that remains of the original structure, save for the abutments still visible next to Blackfriars Station, and the Grade II listed abutment on the south bank. St Paul's Station became Blackfriars in February 1937, when the new bridge was also renamed as Blackfriars Railway Bridge, taking the name of its predecessor.

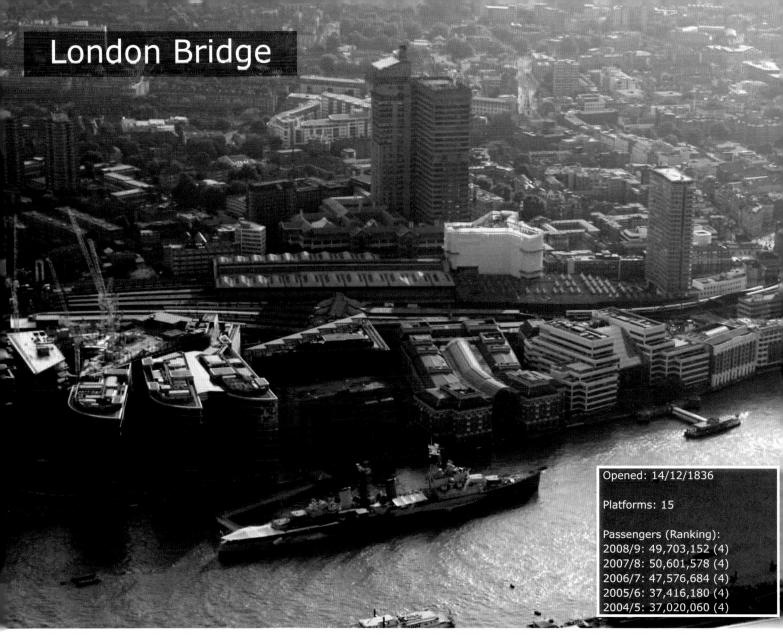

London Bridge

Opened: 14/12/1836

Platforms: 15

Passengers (Ranking):
2008/9: 49,703,152 (4)
2007/8: 50,601,578 (4)
2006/7: 47,576,684 (4)
2005/6: 37,416,180 (4)
2004/5: 37,020,060 (4)

London Bridge has an extremely long and very complicated history. The original station was built by the London & Greenwich Railway (L&GR) in 1836 and had just two platforms. The L&GR struck a deal with another company, the London & Croydon Railway (L&CR), to allow it to use the station. The cost of providing new lines was expensive, so they sold some of the adjacent land to the L&CR for them to build their own station on the north of the site, closer to the riverbank. It opened on June 5th 1839. By 1842 the South Eastern Railway (SER) and the London & Brighton Railway (L&BR) were using this new station. The lines built for their services were on the southern side of the existing tracks, and so the possibility of collisions with L&GR services was very real, as they had to cross over. The rival companies therefore agreed to swap stations, with the L&GR moving to the 1839 station closer to the river, whilst the other three rebuilt the 1836 site into a joint station. With pressure building on the lines due to increases in traffic, a deal was agreed between the L&CR

and the SER to build their own station at Bricklayer's Arms, opening in July 1844, leaving just the L&GR and the L&BR at London Bridge. The L&GR were the main culprits, as the tolls they charged for using their lines into the stations were too high. With the new station came a loss revenue, and the L&GR was absorbed into the SER in 1845 with heavy debts. In 1846 the L&BR and the L&CR merged into the London, Brigh & South Coast Railway (LB&SCR), meaning there were now just two companies using the relevant stations. The SER decide to rebuild the northern 1839 site from 1847-1850, closing the Bricklayer's Arms station, and the LB&SCR built a new terminus on the south side in January 1851. They subsequently demolished this in 1853, and rebuilt again in 1866. Meanwhile, the SER rebuilt their station in 1864 with ne through platforms (far right). When all had settled down, the whole station complex finally became the property of the Southern Railway in 1923. It was completely rebuilt again from 1972-1978.

London Cannon Street

Opened: 01/09/1866

Platforms: 7

Passengers (Ranking):
2008/9: 21,646,380 (12)
2007/8: 22,044,568 (9)
2006/7: 21,106,127 (9)
2005/6: 17,613,560 (11)
2004/5: 17,460,399 (11)

annon Street station is now almost unrecognisable from its original esign. The most instantly noticeably features are the two 120ft towers ther side of the platforms, which is more or less the only remains of the original station. Opened by the South Eastern in 1866 following 3 ears of construction, the towers flanked a magnificent glazed iron-rched roof, 120ft tall and 680ft long. At the northern end of the site as a superb hotel, which opened a year later in 1867, and a 90ft recourt. Originally there were 9 platforms, including one small bay Platform No. 4). The bay platform was removed following edevelopment works in 1926, which also saw the bridge strengthened allow use by heavier locomotives, but the station was to suffer heavy amage during World War II. The roof was badly hit during the air raids f May 10th and 11th 1941, in which the hotel was also damaged. The

glazing was destroyed, but the iron structure was left standing. Sadly, it was not to last, and was demolished from April 1958-January 1959, producing over 1000 tons of metal for scrap. The hotel lasted until 1963 when the station was redeveloped again. It was replaced by a new office block, which is itself currently being redeveloped. The platforms, of which there are now 7 following refurbishment works in 1990, were submerged under a somewhat grotesque office development in 1988 after the "Air Rights" to the space above the station were sold off. This gave extra protection for passengers from the elements, but created a much darker and constricted atmosphere inside the station.

London Charing Cross

Opened: 11/01/1864

Platforms: 6

Passengers (Ranking):
2008/9: 36,659,932 (5)
2007/8: 36,294,182 (5)
2006/7: 34,779,287 (5)
2005/6: 28,562,268 (6)
2004/5: 28,822,074 (5)

Another South Eastern station that no longer resembles its original design, Charing Cross has also sold off its air rights for an office development, but unlike Cannon Street the quality of the design is far superior. The station was designed by the famous railway engineer Sir John Hawkshaw, who also designed Cannon Street Station. When it opened it featured a single span, wrought-iron roof measuring 164ft by 510ft, and was entered by a new wrought-iron rail bridge. Named Hungerford Bridge, it replaced a suspension footbridge built by Isambard Kingdom Brunel in 1845, which was purchased by the SER and demolished. The station was built to enable passengers from Kent to travel right into the heart of London City Centre, meaning the line was extended over the Thames from London Bridge Station on the south bank. A year after its opening, a fine hotel was also opened to the north of the platforms, fronting The Strand. The station roof was not to last long. A 70ft section collapsed on December 5th 1905, requiring it to be rebuilt. The new structure was a ridge and furrow design and was the same size as the original. It lasted until the late 1980s when a major new office development was constructed over the station. Known as Embankment Place, work started on the offices in 1988 and was finished in 1992, at a cost of around £130m. Not all of the roof was dismantled however, and the northern two bays were retained over the main station concourse. The glazed ridge and furrow design can just be see on the right hand side of the image, between the offices and the rear of the hotel. In 2002 the Hungerford Bridge was extended on either side with the addition of two new 13ft wide footbridges, which helped to strengthen the original foundations. The footbridges are noticeable by their white leaning support pylons either side of the iron latticework.

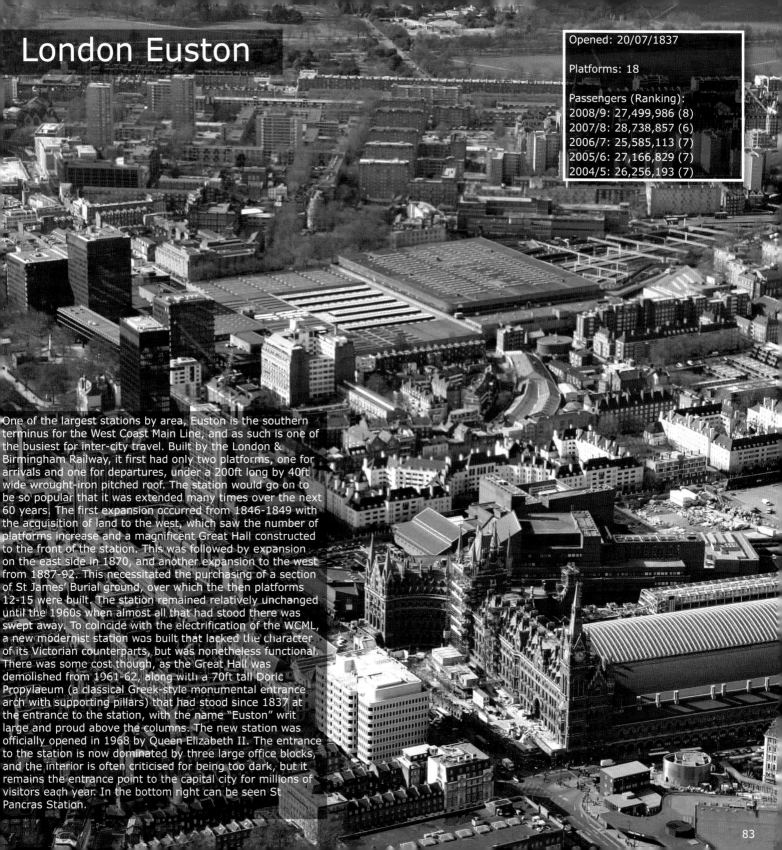

London Euston

Opened: 20/07/1837

Platforms: 18

Passengers (Ranking):
2008/9: 27,499,986 (8)
2007/8: 28,738,857 (6)
2006/7: 25,585,113 (7)
2005/6: 27,166,829 (7)
2004/5: 26,256,193 (7)

One of the largest stations by area, Euston is the southern terminus for the West Coast Main Line, and as such is one of the busiest for inter-city travel. Built by the London & Birmingham Railway, it first had only two platforms, one for arrivals and one for departures, under a 200ft long by 40ft wide wrought-iron pitched roof. The station would go on to be so popular that it was extended many times over the next 60 years. The first expansion occurred from 1846-1849 with the acquisition of land to the west, which saw the number of platforms increase and a magnificent Great Hall constructed to the front of the station. This was followed by expansion on the east side in 1870, and another expansion to the west from 1887-92. This necessitated the purchasing of a section of St James' Burial ground, over which the then platforms 12-15 were built. The station remained relatively unchanged until the 1960s when almost all that had stood there was swept away. To coincide with the electrification of the WCML, a new modernist station was built that lacked the character of its Victorian counterparts, but was nonetheless functional. There was some cost though, as the Great Hall was demolished from 1961-62, along with a 70ft tall Doric Propylaeum (a classical Greek-style monumental entrance arch with supporting pillars) that had stood since 1837 at the entrance to the station, with the name "Euston" writ large and proud above the columns. The new station was officially opened in 1968 by Queen Elizabeth II. The entrance to the station is now dominated by three large office blocks, and the interior is often criticised for being too dark, but it remains the entrance point to the capital city for millions of visitors each year. In the bottom right can be seen St Pancras Station.

London Fenchurch Street

Fenchurch Street was built by the London & Blackwall Railway as a new terminus for its line into the City. It effectively replaced the old terminus station of Minories, which had opened in July 1840 just to the south. Fenchurch Street opened a year later in 1841. Minories lasted until 1854 when Fenchurch was expanded, meaning it was no longer required. The original station by Sir William Tite gained a new roof in the rebuild. Measuring 300ft long by 105 feet wide, it was a segmental trussed arch roof, built in a single span. The existing façade was also constructed at this time, an elegant grey brick structure with curved roof and 11 round-arched windows. The station roof lasted until 1983 when it was removed and replaced by a new office building over the main concourse area (far right). A second much larger block (One America Square, centre) was completed over the platforms in 1990. Of particular note in the image is the small barrel roof next to the approaches on the far left. This is Tower Gateway Station on the Docklands Light Railway, and is built on the exact spot of the original Minories Station. It opened in 1987 as the terminus for the original DLR line into the City. The small station has two platforms, but was rebuilt as a single-track line between June 2008 and March 2009. Here it is seen during the reconstruction, as there are no tracks visible on the left. Previously there had been two tracks either side of an island platform.

Opened: 20/07/1841

Platforms: 4

Passengers (Ranking):
2008/9: 15,675,602 (20)
2007/8: 16,210,539 (17)
2006/7: 15,188,941 (16)
2005/6: 15,746,318 (15)
2004/5: 16,086,112 (13)

Located in the very heart of the City of London is Liverpool Street Station, the third busiest in the UK. The station is now surrounded by the modern towers of the financial district, but much of the original buildings have been retained following a major rebuild in 1992. When it opened in 1874 it was the London terminus for the Great Eastern Railway, and within a year it had 9 operational platforms. The GER's previous terminus has been at Shoreditch, which opened in July 1840. This was subsequently renamed as Bishopsgate to give the impression that it was closer to the city, but with the opening of Liverpool Street the station became superfluous, and it closed to passengers on November 1st 1875, later becoming a goods depot. Liverpool Street Station was enlarged in 1894 with the addition of a new eastern shed, which was completed on April 2nd. This shed was to be sacrificed many years later when a huge redevelopment of the surrounding area commenced. Known as the Broadgate development, an area of over 32 acres was rebuilt into a large complex of offices. The eastern shed was removed and a new office block built above it (visible on the middle left) but the original western shed was retained and restored. One major casualty was the adjacent Broad Street Station, which had predated Liverpool Street. Opened on November 1st 1865, the station closed in 1986 in readiness for the Broadgate development. Broad Street had a total of 9 platforms under a twin pitched roof, with some further sidings on the western side. Today, there is no trace left of the station (in the lower right).

Opened: 02/02/1874

Platforms: 18

Passengers (Ranking):
2008/9: 55,103,416 (3)
2007/8: 57,759,809 (3)
2006/7: 55,265,748 (3)
2005/6: 47,271,234 (3)
2004/5: 50,469,209 (2)

London Liverpool Street

If any station can be described as the "poster station" of the Victorian era, then it is St Pancras. The station features two masterpieces of Victorian design and engineering, but it came so close to being demolished. It was opened by the Midland Railway in 1868, who had previously operated their services out of Euston and King's Cross. The company had been buying land in the area since 1861, and after clashing with the Great Northern Railway (who owned King's Cross) over capacity restrictions in 1862, the ball was started rolling on their own terminus on a line from Bedford to London. The result was a magnificent 689ft by 243ft glass and iron train shed, the largest single span shed of any kind in the world at that time. With an interior height of 100ft, it was airy and spacious. Designed by William Henry Barlow with help from Rowland Mason Ordish, the roof was the crowning glory of the station, which had been built by the Midland to be the most impressive in the capital. Barlow was the man responsible for the planning of the station, and it was his idea to raise the level of the incoming approaches by almost 20ft on large iron columns, thus creating an enormous amount of space underneath. This would later be utilised for storing beer barrels, amongst other things.

Opened: 01/10/1868

Platforms: 13

Passengers (Ranking):
2008/9: 17,462,297 (18)*
2007/8: 6,623,321 (40)
2006/7: 5,777,188 (48)
2005/6: 4,893,313 (46)
2004/5: 5,471,621 (41)

*(Includes King's Cross Thameslink)

The next masterpiece to be built was the Midland Grand Hotel at the front of the station, a huge gothic revival building with 300 rooms. Designed by George Gilbert Scott from 1868-1876, the hotel came in over budget at £428,000 (close to £30m in today's money). The station suffered bomb damage in World War II but survived, only for it to be faced with demolition in 1966. After much campaigning, particularly by the poet Sir John Betjeman, the station was reprieved, and a year later the entire complex was given Grade I listed status by English Heritage. In 2001 work started on transforming the station for the 21st century. The station was rebuilt and the original Victorian features restored at a cost of almost £800m in preparation for the arrival of Eurostar services. The shed was reglazed and painted, and new extra long platforms were built stretching 1493 feet (almost 498 yards) in order to accommodate the new trains. This required a new 656ft shed to be built at the back of the original. The new station was fitted with 13 platforms, with the Eurostar using the middle six. The undercroft used for storing beer barrels has also been converted into a large concourse and departure lounge with many retail units and cafes. The station officially reopened on November 6th 2007 as "St Pancras International". The old hotel is also being redeveloped as a 5* Mariott, with the upper floors forming luxury flats. As part of the redevelopment, a new Thameslink station was built below ground to replace the old King's Cross Thameslink station on the other side of th street. This has resulted in the total number of passengers using the station soaring to almost 18 million at the last count.

London St Pancras
& London King's Cross

Opened: 14/10/1852

Platforms: 12

Passengers (Ranking):
2008/9: 24,641,427 (10)
2007/8: 23,945,017 (8)
2006/7: 22,503,777 (8)
2005/6: 20,301,663 (10)
2004/5: 20,805,979 (9)

Somewhat overshadowed by its more prominent neighbour, King's Cross is itself undergoing a major redevelopment. Opened by the Great Northern to be their main London terminus on the East Coast Main Line, the station predates St Pancras by 16 years and is of an entirely different style. The first GNR station was a temporary affair at Maiden Lane, opening in August 1850. Its replacement was built at a cost of £123,500 (excluding land costs of £65,000) and was designed by Lewis Cubitt. The buildings featured an 800ft long shed with two separate arch vaults, each 105ft wide. The main entrance was marked with a clock tower either side of huge glazed semi-circular windows that mirrored the shape of the roof behind. On the west of the station, in between King's cross and St Pancras, is the Great Northern Hotel. Also designed by Cubitt, this opened on May 17th 1854. The land to

the rear of the station is also important, as this housed various goods sheds and yards, including Cubitt's 1850 Western Transit Shed. This whole site is now part of the 67 acre King's Cross Central development, that will see over 2,000 new homes, 5.25million sq ft of offices, retail space and new public squares. Part of the transit shed will become a university campus. The station itself is being refurbished at a cost of £500m. Due to open by 2013, the work will see the unloved 1971 concourse at the front of the building removed (the low, black structure) to reveal more of the original Grade I listed façade. There will also be a major new concourse on the western side, construction of which can already be seen in this photograph to the left of the station, with one additional platform within the station.

Vauxhall

Although it is one of London's less celebrated stations, Vauxhall is still an important through station on the line to Waterloo. It is situated in the borough of Lambeth on the south bank of the River Thames, and is just 200 yards north west of the Oval cricket ground. The station sits alongside the extremely busy Vauxhall Cross junction, where six large roads meet. Along with the adjacent bus station, the site is an important transport interchange in London, and it is also the southernmost entry point to the road congestion charging zone. Opened by the London & South Western Railway, Vauxhall Station replaced the terminus at Nine Elms when the line was extended into Waterloo in 1848. The station featured a fine building designed by Sir William Tite with a five arch porte cochere, but it was damaged during an air raid in 1941 and demolished in the 1960s. It is now the site of New Covent Garden Market, just south east of Battersea Power Station. Much of the line into Vauxhall Station is elevated above street level, and this can be seen by the presence of the viaduct upon which the station sits, with arches visible on both the left and the right of the picture. Despite this, the ticket office is at ground level (centre). When it was first built the station consisted of only one island platform, but by 1896 this had been extended to three islands, providing a total of 6 platforms. The platform at the very south of the station (top) was the last to be added. Also of note is the building in the foreground, which is the headquarters of MI

London Victoria

Opened: 01/10/1860

Platforms: 19

Passengers (Ranking):
2008/9: 70,157,115 (2)
2007/8: 70,854,435 (2)
2006/7: 66,749,335 (2)
2005/6: 47,859,728 (2)
2004/5: 48,046,867 (3)

Victoria is another station with a complex history, and is the result of two separate termini built by a collection of different companies. The London, Brighton & South Coast (LB&SCR), The Great Western (GWR), The London & North Western (LNWR) and The East Kent Railway (EKR), were all searching for a place to build a line over the Thames and into Westminster from the south. Between them they formed the "Victoria Station & Pimlico Railway Company", with the aim of extending the line from the recent LB&SCR station at Battersea Wharf over the river. Permission was granted for the line in July 1859, but with construction underway the LB&SCR made an attempt to absorb the VS&PR. When this bill was defeated following objections from the GWR and the LC&DR, it was agreed that a second terminus station would be built next door for the other three companies. In the interim, they would be able to use the first terminus until their station was completed. The LB&SCR station opened on October 1st 1860 on the western side of the site (top). At the front of the building the superb Grosvenor Hotel would open in 1861, providing an elegant frontage to the station. It was later purchased by the LB&SCR in 1899. The EKR (known as the London, Chatham & Dover Railway from August 1st 1859) opened their station next door on August 25th 1862. It featured a roof with two arched vaults, the western being 127ft by 455ft, and the eastern 129ft by 385ft. The LB&SCR station was demolished and rebuilt in 1906. The Southern Railway was to absorb all of the constituent companies involved in the VS&PR in 1923 and united the two stations as one in 1924 with the removal of the interior wall between them. From the air their original distinctiveness can still be seen near the northern end (far right), but much of the central part of the station is now covered by the Victoria Place Shopping Centre (centre), which was built from 1980-1985, and a further office block on the southern end (left).

Waterloo is by for the largest station in Great Britain. It has more platforms than any other, with 24. It has more passengers than any other, with close to 90 million per year, and it covers the largest area of any station, with over 25 acres of land. The station was designed by William Tite for the London & South Western Railway, when the line was extended from Nine Elms via Vauxhall. The original intention was for Waterloo to be a through station to the City, but it would ultimately end up being a terminus. It opened as "Waterloo Bridge Station" in 1848, being named for the nearby bridge over the river, but the name of just "Waterloo" stuck with the locals and this was officially adopted in 1886. The station was less than perfect, with a confusing array of platforms, platform numbers and poor signage that would result in it being completely rebuilt by the L&SWR between 1900 and 1922. Work was carried out in stages, being delayed by the passage of the First World War, but when it was completed the station had 21 platforms and a huge glazed ridge and furrow roof, measuring 520ft by 540 ft.

The façade and buildings at the front were built out of Portland Stone and featured the "Victory Arch" (bottom right). This was built from 1919-1922 to commemorate soldiers from the L&SWR and the Southern Railway who had died during the Great War. It now also commemorates those lost during World War II. The arch is the main entrance into the station and since March 2002 it has been Grade II listed. In the 1990s the station was to undergo another major redevelopment when platforms 20 and 21 were demolished to make way for the new Waterloo International Station that would be the terminus for Eurostar services from France. The station would feature 5 extra long platforms with a 1312ft snake-like roof (on the right). The total cost of the station was £135m. It was ready by May 1993, and officially opened on November 14th 1994 when the first cross-channel service ran. The International station is now closed after the Eurostar transferred to St Pancras in 2007. The platforms are not currently being used and may need further conversion work if they are to be able to accept main line train services.

Opened: 11/07/1848

Platforms: 24

Passengers (Ranking):
2008/9: 87,930,076 (1)
2007/8: 91,452,130 (1)
2006/7: 83,993,314 (1)
2005/6: 61,036,093 (1)
2004/5: 62,388,929 (1)

London Waterloo

Willesden Junction

site with a huge amount of history, this image shows two active stations, one former station, a maintenance depot, a freight depot built on the site of an old maintenance depot, and the site of a huge former carriage shed. The line running from bottom-left to top-right is the West Coast Main Line. In the centre, in between the rail and road bridges can be seen the remains of Willesden Junction (Main Line) Station. Opened on September 1st 1866 by the London & North Western, this station originally had 2 platforms. On September 2nd 1867 the North London Railway opened a station immediately to the south end of Willesden Junction, with the track and platforms passing over the main line. This became known as Willesden High Level Station (centre right). This station was rebuilt, opening again in August 1894 with a new platform subsequently demolished around 1956). A third station opened on June 5th 1912 on the north side, called Willesden Junction New (now Willesden Low Level Station"). This was built alongside the original Main Line station, and featured 4 platforms (2 through and 2 bay). Soon

after, in October 1915, London Underground trains began to use this station as part of the Bakerloo Line. By 1962 Willesden Main Line Station had acquired a total of 9 platforms (7 through, 2 bay), but the station was due for closure due to the electrification of the WCML. The platforms were lifted to enable realignment of the tracks, and the station shut on December 3rd. Today, the Low Level and High Level stations are regarded as one station with 5 platforms (one of the low level bays is no longer used). In 2008/9 the combined station had a total of 1.2m overground passengers, and 3.5m underground passengers. In the bottom middle of the image is Willesden T.M.D, built around 1965 to replace the old LNWR depot just to the north. This was redeveloped as a freight depot (top right, with the large yellow cranes). The new depot has a 6-track shed, and a refuelling side. On the left of the image is the site of the huge former London, Midland & Scottish carriage shed, which had 24 entrance tracks. The land is now a waste processing centre.

Hornsey is an area of north west London just west of Tottenham. Here there is a large maintenance depot and a small, rather unimpressive main line station (lower middle, under the shorter footbridge).

The station was opened on August 7th 1850 by the Great Northern Railway on the London to York Line. The work of William Cubitt, the original station was built in near pristine countryside and featured two platforms, as it still does today.

The site was to develop quickly into a large rail facility. By 1896 there were substantial sidings on both the Up and Down sides of the track, known as Ferme Park Sidings. Over the next 20 years these would increase hugely, with a new engine shed built on the eastern Up side. This is the existing red-brick shed on the left. The sidings were extended north on the Down side where further sheds were built next to what is now Cranford Way (far right). Much of this site is now an industrial estate.

The large shed in the centre of the image is part of Hornsey Traction & Rolling Stock Maintenance Depot. Run by First Capital Connect, the shed services trains for the Thameslink routes across the whole of London.

There are plans to create a new depot just to the north of the site (left of picture) to enable further Thameslink maintenance. The new depot would feature a 920ft, 8-track shed capable of holding 12-car trains, as well as a new washing shed and sidings.

Hornsey T.M.D.

Old Oak Common

his historic site was the location of the Great Western Railway's main ondon Locomotive Works. The GWR needed a new site for a much rger depot after the expansion of Paddington Station, which started in ?06. They chose this site in north London just north west of Acton, on e opposite side of Wormwood Scrubs. The 1838 GWR main line from addington runs immediately between the two on the left side of the cture, heading towards the top right. The new GWR depot opened on arch 17th 1906, and the location of the original buildings is on the ght hand side. Here we can see some of the remaining sheds, cluding the last operational turntable. This used to be housed inside a ant locomotive shed along with three other turntables. Up until immer 2009 this part of the site was owned by DB Schenker Rail (UK) reviously known as English, Welsh & Scottish Railway, or EWS, before

being taken over), who are the largest rail freight company in the UK. The site is currently vacant, and the remaining buildings are due for demolition. The buildings in the middle of the site are the First Great Western high speed train depots, built on the location of the old GWR carriage shed. On the left of the image, on the opposite side of the GWR main line, is North Pole Depot, which was home to the Eurostar trains from 1994 until 2007. In 2010 Old Oak Common was identified as a possible site for a future high speed rail station as part of "High Speed 2", a major new high speed link to the north via Birmingham. It has also been identified as the possible site of a station under the London "Crossrail" proposals. As yet, neither of these plans has been confirmed, and the future of the site is still to be decided.

Selhurst T.M.D.

The 38 acre Selhurst Depot is located in South London by the Norwood fork of the old London, Brighton & South Coast Railway lines. It is now operated by Southern Railways and has recently undergone a major £50m upgrade. The first sidings had appeared in the site by 1896 but the first major buildings weren't to follow until after 1915, when the depot was first developed. A large 12-track cleaning shed was opened (bottom left with the three pitched roof arches) with an electrical repair shed in the centre of the site. The depot continued to develop over the years and was used to maintain the new electric EMU's by the 1950s, as well as all manner of locomotives, wagons and carriages. In 1986 a new large inspection shed was opened (centre right, with red stripes on the roof) for the Class 455 rolling stock built at York. This was the last major development until 2006. The updated depot now features a new repair shop (bottom middle, on the right of the 1920s cleaning shed) and has 9 new train parking roads capable of holding 108 train carriages (centre). There is also a carriage washer (top left) and driver training zone, which includes a train simulator.

Temple Mills Depot

This is the site of the new Eurostar depot in Leyton, north west London. Built at an overall cost of £402million, the huge shed replaces the old North Pole Depot at Old Oak Common. It was decided to move the maintenance of the Eurostar trains as accessing the old depot would have proved difficult from the new high-speed rail link ("High Speed 1"). The total costs included the price for land, a new spur from the nearby Stratford International Station at the Olympic Park site, and costs associated with relocating from North Pole Depot, as well as the new shed.

The new shed sits by the side of the Great Eastern Railway's Cambridge line and features 8 train roads. It is an enormous 1427ft long, by 177ft wide, designed to accommodate the lengthy Eurostar trains. From the air the new building now competes for attention with the equally impressive building on the opposite side of the tracks. This is New Spitalfields Market. Historically the rail site was home to a GER wagon works, and its previous use before the new depot was as a freight marshalling yard for EWS. The new site is expected to employ around 350 people and officially opened in October 2007.

The name of London Underground is something of a misnomer, as over half of the network is actually above ground (around 55%). As such, there are some quite substantial stations at street level, along with some submerged stations that are open to the elements and thus visible from the air. This is a selection of a few of them.

Bow Road (right, top) is located in Bow, East London. On the District and Hammersmith & City Lines, it is a typical example of a low-level underground station with street-level ticket office. The red brick station building is Grade II listed.

East Finchley (right, bottom), is a former overground station built by the Edgware, Highgate & London Railway (by the time the station opened, the EH&LR had been absorbed by the Great Northern Railway). It was first known as "East End Station", before gaining its current name in 1886. It became part of the underground following the "Northern Heights" plan of 1935 to extend the network using existing rail assets, including overground networks. The old station was rebuilt with an extra island platform in an Art Deco style, and the first Underground service operated from the station in July 1939. The last steam overground service was in March 1941.

Dollis Hill tube station (Opposite page, top left) is in north London, between Willesden and Harlesden. It is on the Jubilee Line, but opened as part of the Metropolitan Line.

Wembley Park Station (Opposite, top right) is one of the largest on the Underground with 6 platforms. It was extended in 1948 when the Olympic Games were held at the nearby Wembley stadium, and it was also recently refurbished when the stadium was rebuilt.

Golders Green (Opposite, Bottom) was the northern terminus for the Charing Cross, Euston & Hampstead Railway. The site also comprised the main depot for the company, which is now the main underground depot on the Northern Line. It became a through station in 1923 when the line was extended. Despite having 5 platforms there are only 3 tracks into the station.

Opened: 02/06/1902

Platforms: 2

2008 Passengers: 5,320,000

Opened: 22/08/1867

Platforms: 4

2008 Passengers: 5.95m

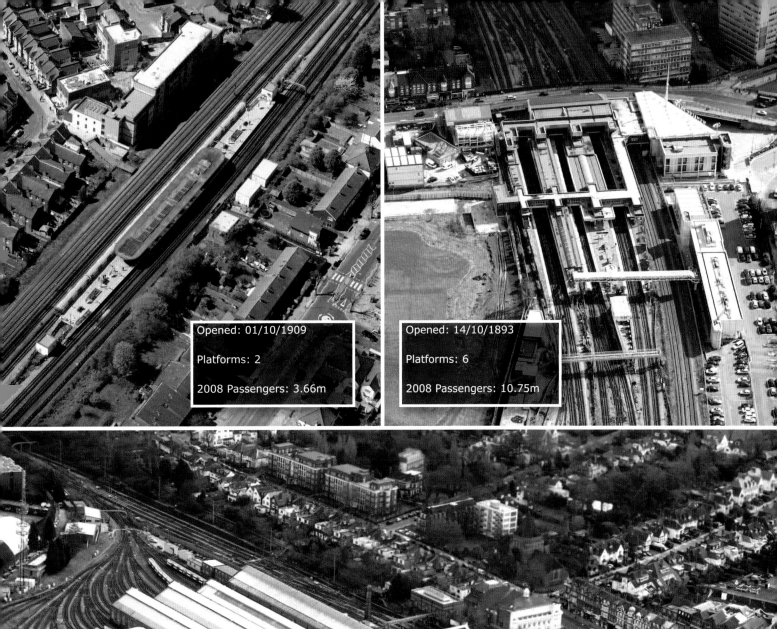

Opened: 01/10/1909

Platforms: 2

2008 Passengers: 3.66m

Opened: 14/10/1893

Platforms: 6

2008 Passengers: 10.75m

Opened: 22/06/1907

Platforms: 5

2008 Passengers: 7.67m

The London Underground was the world's first subterranean railway system, and it is still the largest. The huge fleet of locomotives and carriages on the system therefore need regular servicing and maintenance, resulting in the need for several large depots throughout London.

On the right is Northumberland Park Depot in north east London. This is the main depot for the Victoria Line, and features the only part of the line that isn't underground (the approach tracks heading towards the sheds). The depot opened in April 1968 next to Northumberland Park Station (bottom right). The station was built by the Northern & Eastern Railway, opening on September 15th 1840 as Marsh Lane. By 1915 the site had acquired a good number of sidings, which is now the site of the main depot shed. The depot was refurbished in 2007 at a cost of £15m.

The largest depot on the entire Underground Network is Neasden Depot (opposite page, bottom), just to the east of Wembley Stadium in north west London. It is on the Metropolitan Line, which was the first line to be built in the Underground system. The site was used as a repair works for the Metropolitan Railway. In 2008 a £75m redevelopment was started that would include a new repair shed.

Hainault depot (opposite, top) is also in north east London and opened around 1938. It is the largest depot on the Central Line. In the top right of the image is Hainault Tube Station. This opened in May 1903 as an overground station for the Great Eastern Railway. The last steam trains ran on the line in November 1947 before it was converted to Underground services. The depot was used during World War II as a base for the USA Army Transportation Corps. The main carriage shed (centre) and the cleaning shed (right) are the original buildings.

The Docklands Light Railway (or DLR) was built to service the redeveloped docklands area in east London that now forms the UK's second largest financial centre after the City of London. Once the busiest shipping port in the world, the docklands area had practically become defunct by the 1980s and had fallen into decay. The plan to rebuild the area would eventually see huge new office buildings taking shape, such as the famous One Canada Square tower, right, which is currently the tallest building in Britain. In order for people to travel to and from the new development, a new light railway system was constructed. Built at an original cost of around £77m, the railway opened on August 31st 1987. Most of its stations are elevated above street level, with the trains comprising of two cars (soon to be upgraded to three). The original route included Westferry Station (below), which is a typical example of a DLR station. The largest and most spectacular station on the network is Canary Wharf Station, (main image, bottom right) which nestles in between the huge buildings either side. The station features six platforms around three tracks, and is built under a huge arched roof that creates a superb entrance to the main office complex. The station also has direct access to the first floor Cabot's Place Shopping Centre. This station was part of the original 1987 plan and was due to have just two platforms, but when it was realised that demand for access would be huge the station was rebuilt before it could open, finally opening in November 1991.

Loughborough Central

This station is the northern terminus of the preserved Great Central Railway heritage line that runs to Leicester. The GCR had previously been known as the Manchester, Sheffield and Lincolnshire Railway before they changed their name in 1897, when construction started on an extension of the line to London. The station here at Loughborough was to open two years later, but lasted only until 1969. Following the planned closure, a group of enthusiasts formed the "Main Line Station Trust" and set about acquiring the station and some of the line to ensure that steam locomotives could run on original sections of railway, as they had been designed to do.

In the following years Loughborough Central was restored, and further sections of track reopened all of the way south to Leicester North, a distance of 8 miles. There are two further stations on the preserved route, Quorn & Woodhouse, and Rothley. A further section of the original line has also been preserved by the Main Line Station Trust in the Nottingham area.

At Loughborough, the station has been restored to late 1950s style, and now features a museum, refreshment room and gift shop. It is also the site of the line's main loco shed to the north, where the railway's twenty working locomotives are maintained. Some of the rolling stock can just be seen at the top of the image. The preserved Great Central Railway is now the only heritage railway in the UK to operate on main line double track, and is run by a team of 700 volunteers.

Opened: 15/03/1899

Closed: 05.05.1969

Platforms: 2

Macclesfield

Opened: 03/04/1871

Platforms: 4

Passengers (Ranking):
2008/9: 1,133,882 (391)
2007/8: 1,171,280 (358)
2006/7: 1,085,517 (370)
2005/6:   914,884 (326)
2004/5:   713,194 (408)

This was the second major station to be built in the Cheshire town of Macclesfield. The first opened in July 1849 on the newly opened London & North Western route from Manchester. Around the same time, the North Staffordshire Railway opened a section of their route to Stoke between Congleton and Macclesfield. The two lines met in the north of the town where a joint station was built, to be known as Hibel Road. This remained the town's station for 20 years, when the NSR began to look for an alternative route to Manchester in order to avoid paying higher charges to the LNWR, who preferred the NSR traffic to go via the longer route through Crewe. The NSR teamed up with the Manchester, Sheffield & Lincolnshire Railway to build a route to Manchester via Marple, just east of Stockport.

Together they formed the Macclesfield, Bollington & Marple Railway, with the northern terminus at Marple Rose Hill. It opened in August 1869 with a temporary station in Macclesfield, but a new permanent station was to open in 1871 called Macclesfield Central. It was located just 300 yards to the south of Hibel Road and was initially opened for goods traffic only, with passenger services starting on July 1st 1873.

Both stations were to remain in operation until 1960, when British Rail opted to redevelop Central and close Hibel Road. Central became known simply as "Macclesfield", reopening in November that year. Although the station has 4 platforms only 3 are in use due to there being only 3 tracks. The eastern most platform (far right, small image) serves a single track, and is often used as a bay platform for local services that do not travel beyond Macclesfield, even though it reconnects with the rest of the main line further south. The route from Macclesfield to Marple Rose Hll now forms part of the Middlewood Way nature trail that opened in 1985 after the line closed in 1970.

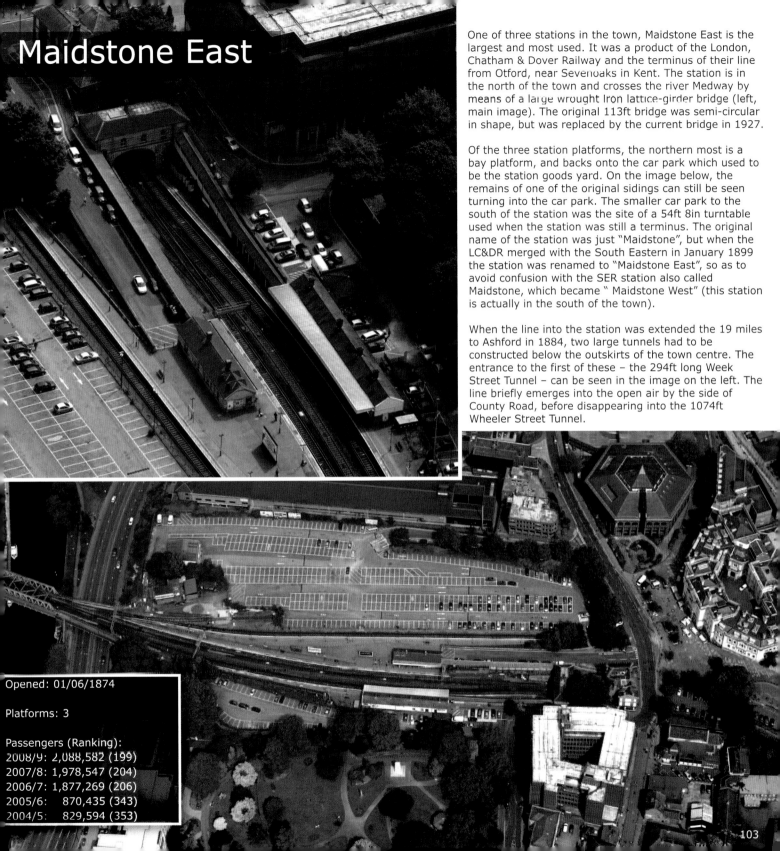

Maidstone East

One of three stations in the town, Maidstone East is the largest and most used. It was a product of the London, Chatham & Dover Railway and the terminus of their line from Otford, near Sevenoaks in Kent. The station is in the north of the town and crosses the river Medway by means of a large wrought Iron lattice-girder bridge (left, main image). The original 113ft bridge was semi-circular in shape, but was replaced by the current bridge in 1927.

Of the three station platforms, the northern most is a bay platform, and backs onto the car park which used to be the station goods yard. On the image below, the remains of one of the original sidings can still be seen turning into the car park. The smaller car park to the south of the station was the site of a 54ft 8in turntable used when the station was still a terminus. The original name of the station was just "Maidstone", but when the LC&DR merged with the South Eastern in January 1899 the station was renamed to "Maidstone East", so as to avoid confusion with the SER station also called Maidstone, which became " Maidstone West" (this station is actually in the south of the town).

When the line into the station was extended the 19 miles to Ashford in 1884, two large tunnels had to be constructed below the outskirts of the town centre. The entrance to the first of these – the 294ft long Week Street Tunnel – can be seen in the image on the left. The line briefly emerges into the open air by the side of County Road, before disappearing into the 1074ft Wheeler Street Tunnel.

Opened: 01/06/1874

Platforms: 3

Passengers (Ranking):
2008/9: 2,088,582 (199)
2007/8: 1,978,547 (204)
2006/7: 1,877,269 (206)
2005/6:   870,435 (343)
2004/5:   829,594 (353)

Manchester Piccadilly
& Manchester Mayfield (disused)

The great industrial city of Manchester will forever be associated with the railways, with the world's first passenger station cited within its boundaries. But the largest of its current stations is here at Piccadilly. Built by the Manchester & Birmingham Railway on the line to Crewe, the station opened as "Store Street" before being renamed four years later as "London Road". This was to be its name for well over a century. The station was designed as a terminus, but two through platforms were added on the western side (right, the modern platforms 13 & 14). Opened on August 1st 1849 by the Manchester, South Junction & Altrincham Railway, these platforms served the line from Altrincham via Oxford Road Station. This included a bridge over the adjacent road, for the entire station was built above street level on large iron columns, thus providing a level gradient for the tracks.

The station was substantially rebuilt around 1866 when the first two spans of the huge iron roof were added. 680ft in length, they were originally mostly clad in slate with some glass sections. The two further spans (on the right) were added around 1881. In the early twentieth century the station had reached full capacity, and a solution to overcrowding was needed. The London & North Western (the successor of the M&BR) decided to build a second station just to the south of London Road. This was to be Manchester Mayfield Station (top right). The new terminus station opened on August 8th 1910 with 5 platforms, a glazed ridge and furrow roof, and a red-brick main entrance building. Like London Road, the station was built above street level and shared the main approach tracks into the city. It was mostly used for suburban services and was to close on August 28th 1960 after 50 years of use. In July 1970 the station reopened as a parcel depot that lasted for 16 years. The station now lies unused and in decay, although there have been plans mooted to reopen it, either as a terminus or a new through route to Oxford Road, to relieve pressure on the already strained Piccadilly. London Road officially became Piccadilly in September 1960 following another period of rebuilding. The large office block to the front of the station was added in 1969 over the concourse area. In the late 1990s the Grade II listed roof was given a major overhaul, which included it being fitted with over 10,000 new toughened glass panels, increasing the amount of light reaching the platforms below. The next major scheme would see the creation of a huge new concourse area replacing the one from the 1960 rebuild. Opened at a cost of over £60m in 2002, the new entrance and waiting area has transformed the interior of the station, creating a fabulous gateway into the city.

Opened: 08/05/1842

Platforms: 14

Passengers (Ranking):
2008/9: 20,132,391 (14)
2007/8: 20,385,279 (12)
2006/7: 14,513,542 (18)
2005/6: 21,230,613 (9)
2004/5: 18,958,922 (10)

Manchester Victoria
& Manchester Exchange (site of)

Manchester Victoria:

Opened: 01/01/1844

Platforms: 8

Passengers* (Ranking):
2008/9: 5,789,892 (51)
2007/8: 4,005,915 (74)
2006/7: 5,060,044 (60)
2005/6:   487,898 (558)
2004/5:   467,297 (566)

*National Rail Only

Victoria was once one of the largest stations in the UK, but it is now a shadow of its former self. At peak operations the station had 17 platforms, but there are just 8 left of which two are used by Metrolink Trams. The station was built by the Manchester & Leeds Railway but for much of its lifetime it was operated by the Lancashire & Yorkshire Railway. The original station was designed by George Stephenson, but the impressive 484ft façade dates from 1909 and is by William Dawes. The platforms behind this façade made up the terminals, whilst the through platforms were on the north side under what is now the M.E.N. Arena (left). This large indoor venue opened in July 1995, creating a dark and claustrophobic environment over the remaining platforms. The main building is still rather grand inside, but dilapidated. The roof was damaged in the IRA bomb of 1996, but it was already falling apart and it is now full of holes. As can be seen from the image, the terminus platforms on the far right have been completely removed and paved over. In May 2010 work was completed on rebuilding platforms 1 & 2, and in August 2010 it was confirmed that the station would receive a £30m investment that would see a new roof fitted. Immediately to the west of Victoria are the remains of Manchester Exchange Station (small image, right). Opened on June 30th 1884, it was built by the LNWR so they wouldn't have to pay for using the L&YR operated Victoria. Despite the name it was actually in Salford on the opposite side of the River Irwell, but it could only be accessed from the Manchester side. The station had 5 platforms, and from 1929 platform 3 (on the left of the small picture) was extended to meet up with Victoria's platform 11, creating a mammoth 2194ft platform, the longest in Europe. The station closed on May 5th 1969 and little now remains, save for the footbridge and remnants of the platforms.

Manchester Central (disused)

Opened: 01/07/1880

Closed: 05/05/1969

Platforms: 9

he magnificent Central Station may no longer be in service, but unlike many that closed due to the Beeching axe its magnificent structure ill stands. Central was opened by the Cheshire Lines Committee, a mpany formed from the Great Northern Railway, the Midland Railway, d the Manchester, Sheffield & Lincolnshire Railway. In 1873 their line Liverpool Central opened, and the need for their own terminus station as therefore created, instead of using the LNWR London Road Station. ork started in 1875 to a design by Sir John Fowler. During construction temporary terminus was to open in 1877 alongside the construction e (right). This would later become a CLC goods depot. When it was ished, Central had 6 platforms underneath a breathtaking single span n roof, measuring 550ft by 210ft, with a height of 90ft in the centre. 1903 the Midland Railway opened their own masterpiece, the Midland

Hotel, directly opposite the station (bottom left). It had been originally planned to be built immediately in front of the station, but was instead built on the opposite side of Windmill Street. In 1906 the station gained 3 new outside platforms on its approaches (top right), taking the total to 9. The station served the city well, meaning Manchester had three major termini in the city centre. However, it was deemed surplus to requirements in 1969, and closed on May 5th. Just a decade earlier, there had been over 1 million outgoing passengers in 1959. The station then fell into disrepair. It was used as a car park up until 1978, when it was bought by the then Greater Manchester County Council, who converted it into a major exhibition venue known as the GMEX (Greater Manchester Exhibition Centre). Since June 2007 the name of the centre has been "Manchester Central" to reflect its railway heritage.

The world's oldest passenger station, Liverpool Road Station was the eastern terminus of the Liverpool & Manchester Railway. Built by George Stephenson, the station was opened by the Prime Minister, the Duke of Wellington, on September 15th 1830, although the celebrations were overshadowed by the death of the Liverpool MP William Huskisson. He was run over by the "Rocket" locomotive on the journey from Liverpool after alighting to converse with the Duke, who was on a separate train (the "Northumbrian"). He died later in hospital in Eccles. Stephenson's Rocket, built by his son Robert, had triumphed at the Rainhill Trails south of St Helens in October 1829, which were held to find a suitable locomotive for the new line. The site for the station had originally been planned to be on the Salford side of the Irwell (left), but the L&MR wanted it on the Manchester side, and a site was found on Liverpool Road. An existing house, dating from 1808 on the corner of Water Street and Liverpool Road, was bought and would become the superintendent's office (left centre). The new station building was built next door (the sandstone coloured building), and on the opposite side of the tracks a large goods warehouse was constructed. The rail line was level with the first storey of the buildings. In 1831 a carriage shed was built next to the station building (exact centre) with shops at street level below. Despite the ignominious start the station was to prove so successful that several more goods warehouse were built on the site by the late 1830s, along with a transit shed in 1831 (far right) and a new separate arrivals platform on the northern side of Water Street (far left, on the small viaduct, directly after where the branch line separates). The other large brick warehou at the top of the image were built later, with the Grape Street Bonded Goods Warehouse (top centre) opening in 1869. The station only laste for 14 years, and all services were transferred to the new Victoria Station in 1844. However, Liverpool Road continued as a goods statior under the auspices of the LNWR. It was to last until 1975 when it clos Part of the site, including the Grape Street Warehouse, was bought by Granada Studios and now includes the set of Coronation Street on sor of the former sidings (top right). The remainder of the site was bough by Greater Manchester County Council in 1978, reopening in 1983 as Museum Of Science & Industry. Today, the main buildings have been restored, and visitors can experience a trip on a replica "Planet" class locomotive, which was introduced in 1830 to run on the railway.

Manchester Oxford Road

Opened: 20/07/1849

Platforms: 5

Passengers (Ranking):
2008/9: 5,067,434 (62)
2007/8: 1,249,725 (334)
2006/7: 4,330,755 (70)
2005/6:   625,010 (475)
2004/5:   561,701 (502)

s is probably the least well known of Manchester's stations, but architecturally it is considered to be one of the best in the country. It opened on the line from Altrincham by the Manchester, South ction & Altrincham Railway as the original terminus of the route. s was short lived however, as the remainder of the line through to island platform at Manchester London Road opened less than 2 eks later. Oxford Road was considerably rebuilt in 1874 when the out was increased to include 3 through platforms with 2 bay forms on a separate spur (top right). There were also two sidings in ween the bay platforms. The current building dates from 1960 and is de II listed. Its striking appearance includes three overlapping crete shells on the roof, reminiscent of Sydney Opera House, with a inated timber interior suspended on the underside. The platforms

also feature arched canopies in timber with wooden supports, and wooden benches throughout. Oxford Road is described by English Heritage as having a "unique main station building of outstanding architectural quality and technological interest". The new station building reopened on November 12th 1960. An extra platform was added in 1969 following the closure of Manchester Central. This was built on the site of the southern most through line (far left) and took the number of through platforms to four. At the same time one of the bay platforms was closed, although it is still extant and could be reopened in the future. Due to its location right in the heart of the city, Oxford Road is extremely well used and is a convenient stopping off point for commuters.

When the last tram service in Manchester ran in 1949 it marked the end of an era. At its peak the Manchester Corporation Tramway had carried over 300 million passengers in a single year, but after 1949 it was deemed to be surplus to requirements. It wasn't until 1992 that trams returned to the streets of Manchester with the opening of the Metrolink system. Utilising old British Rail routes into the city from Altrincham to Piccadilly, and Bury to Victoria, along with new tracks in Manchester City Centre, the new tramway was to prove a huge success. In December 1999 a third route to Salford Quays opened, being extended to Eccles in July 2000. Here we can see one of the original class T-68 trams in Piccadilly Gardens station (below) on route to Piccadilly, where there is a station in the undercroft below the mainline platforms. From within Piccadilly, this gives the impression that the Metrolink is underground, when it is actually at street level. Whilst most of the stations on the network are similar to the one below, the most striking is the spectacular Central Park Station (bottom right), which was completed in 2005 but is as yet unused. Located in Newton Heath to the north east of the city centre, the station features a copper roof supported by a cable-tension steel pillar. It was due to be a part of the "big bang" expansion on the route to Rochdale and Oldham, but this did not happen as originally planned. However, in August 2010 it was confirmed that funding was in place for the project, which would also see routes to Ashton Under Lyne, South Manchester (Chorlton and East Didsbury) and Manchester Airport. The Queens Road Depot (top right) in Cheetham Hill, to the north of the city, is one of the main Metrolink servicing and stabling areas. It was built on the site of the old Corporation Tramway depot that opened in June 1900. This has recently been upgraded at a cost of £10.5m and now has room for a total of 44 trams.

Margate

Opened: 05/10/1863

Platforms: 4

Passengers (Ranking):
2008/9: 653,152 (607)
2007/8: 671,790 (552)
2006/7: 660,439 (529)
2005/6: 595,453 (491)
2004/5: 584,569 (484)

he original station at Margate was built by the Kent Coast Railway ompany, just yards from the shoreline in the seaside resort. The ompany had previously been known as the "Herne Bay & Faversham ailway" from 1857-1859 and the "Margate Railway" from 1859-1861, nd was involved with constructing several lines around the north Kent ast. It was later to become part of the London, Chatham & Dover ailway in 1871. The original station, known as "Margate C&D", featured platforms (2 through and 1 bay) and also a goods yard. The yard ccupied the land that had first been earmarked for the station, on the ntre left of the photo. It featured a 108ft engine shed, 168ft goods ed and a 45ft turntable. The sidings reached as far as the last row of ouses in the top centre, on what is now the car park. The reason for oving the site was due to the fact that the KCRC had gained ermission to extend the line on to Ramsgate, but could not as there as an earlier station blocking the route. This was Margate SER (from

1899 known as "Margate Sands"), which was located in the top right of this image, immediately behind the modern multi-storey building. The new site allowed a curved station to be built that could avoid the South Eastern Railway's station. In 1899 the station became known as "Margate West", and this changed to simply "Margate" when Margate Sands was closed in 1926. The station was rebuilt in 1912 and extended to 5 platforms with one bay, and the track into the goods yard was shortened and converted into a parcel depot. This dock platform still exists, and can be seen on the left with the asymmetrical brown roof. There were also 5 large sidings and a 59ft turntable on the west side (centre bottom). This is now a housing estate, next to the existing platforms. The bay platform on this side was also removed with the development. The main station building on the opposite side was added in 1926. It features a magnificent, semi-circular booking hall behind its 265ft façade, and is Grade II listed.

Middlesbrough

Opened: 04/06/1846

Platforms: 2

Passengers (Ranking):
2008/9: 1,349,420 (321)
2007/8: 1,300,713 (322)
2006/7: 1,242,054 (318)
2005/6: 1,200,737 (256)
2004/5: 1,120,781 (266)

The railways in Middlesbrough are heavily linked to the original 1825 Stockton & Darlington Railway. In 1831 a branch line was opened to the west of the town that terminated at the Middlesbrough Docks, allowing coal and goods to be shipped with great ease from the huge sidings that developed. This new line enabled the development of the town, which was still a small rural hamlet, to begin in earnest. The first station on the line was built in 1837, but this was demolished and replaced with a station on the existing site in 1846 as part of the Middlesbrough & Redcar Railway. The present structures date from December 3rd 1877 when the station was rebuilt. Designed by William Peachey and WJ Cudworth, the impressive stone buildings are now Grade II listed and originally had a huge iron and glass arched roof over the platforms. Part of the roof was supported on the white ornate iron Albert Bridge, which spans the street called Exchange Square in the centre. The roof was almost completely destroyed in a German air raid on August 3rd 1942, with the falling debris burying a locomotive and crushing the carriages behind. Seven people died in the raid, but within two days the track had been repaired and reopened for service. The iron remnants of the roof remained in place until 1954 when it was finally demolished. In July 1960 a hideous 4-storey British Rail building opened over the Victorian station buildings called Zetland House, helping to ruin the view from all angles. This was finally demolished in 2006 and a new wing added to the station in a style more becoming of the original (top left). The station currently operates with 2 platforms with 2 avoiding freight lines on the north side. The remains of an old bay platform can be seen on the northern side (right), which is now covered by greenery.

Newark Northgate

Opened: 01/08/1852

Platforms: 3

Passengers (Ranking):
2008/9:   960,948 (460)
2007/8:   923,070 (444)
2006/7: 1,187,545 (335)
2005/6:   400,286 (652)
2004/5:   377,172 (665)

This is the busiest of Newark's two stations and is situated in the north west of the town, away from the town centre. It was ...ened in 1852 by the Great Northern Railway as part of their main ...don to Doncaster route. Today it forms part of the East Coast Main ...c. The other station, Newark Castle, predates Northgate by six ...rs, opening in August 1846. This was a Midland station situated on ... north eastern side of town, on the opposite side of the River Trent. ... two lines cross at a point just to the north of Newark at an unusual ...t crossing", where neither track passes over the other. This crossing ... the potential to create delays on the ECML, as high speed trains ...ng it must slow down to ensure a smooth transit over the tracks.

Northgate today is small, but functional. The main station building is mostly single storey and has been Grade II listed since May 1988. There are currently three platforms, but there was a fourth bay platform on the lower western side (bottom right). The platform awning still exists next to the station building (right centre) but the track has since been lifted. The car park in front of the station was previously the site of several sidings and a small goods shed, accessed from a spur further down the track (right, off image). The sidings on the eastern side of the tracks are still extant (top left and centre) but are now becoming overgrown. The curved line of trees on the middle right marks the exact line of a spur to the Great Northern Brickworks that is listed on the 1886 OS map of the town.

Newcastle Central

Opened: 29/08/1850

Platforms: 10 (split into 12)

Passengers (Ranking):
2008/9: 6,800,602 (42)
2007/8: 6,447,267 (43)
2006/7: 6,230,498 (43)
2005/6: 6,108,240 (36)
2004/5: 5,728,348 (38)

The magnificent Grade I listed Central station is undoubtedly one of the finest in Britain. Opened by Queen Victoria in 1850, it was a joint station constructed by the York, Newcastle & Berwick Railway, and the Newcastle & Carlisle Railway. YN&BR trains began using the western end of the station the day after opening on August 30th 1850, and N&CR trains began using the eastern end on January 1st 1851. The main architect for the station was John Dobson, who is famous for his work on the city's Grey Street. There was also considerable input from Robert Stephenson. Stephenson also designed the High Level Bridge over the Tyne that leads into the station's eastern side (opposite page, top left). The bridge, also now Grade I listed and also opened by Queen Victoria, was constructed from 1847-1849 and has an overall span of 1337ft, with a 512ft span over the river. The bridge carries 2 lines of track above, with a pedestrian footway and a single carriage road below, which is now only used by buses and taxis heading south to Gateshead. The original internal layout of Central Station included 4 bay platforms on the eastern side, 3 bay on the west, and 1 through platform along with 5 carriage sidings to the south. This arrangement would allow for several expansions down the years without the need for huge rebuilding. Further platforms were added in place of the sidings in 1871, 1877 and in 1894, when 3 were added the east for suburban services, taking the total to 15. It was at the eastern side where the station featured the world's largest diamond crossing, with dozens of tracks intersecting each other in a complex layout. Most of this crossing has been lifted following the closure of th 1894 suburban platforms. These were largely replaced by the underground Central Station Metro Station, which opened in November 1981. The Tyne & Wear Metro is only the fourth underground system the UK, after London, Glasgow and Liverpool, and now carries around million passengers a year. Today Central station features 10 overgrou platforms, including 5 bays, with the two longest through platforms b split into numbers 5&6 and 7&8, to give a total of 12. The platforms a covered by two separate roof sections. The original 3 bay shed was th first large example of a curved iron-arch roof. The two further sheds t the south were added in 1890 by William Bell. The magnificent entrar building (above) is one of the grandest of any station anywhere. It wa expanded in 1863 by the addition of the central portico, designed by Thomas Prosser, and now makes the perfect entrance to one of the m important stations on the East Coast Main Line.

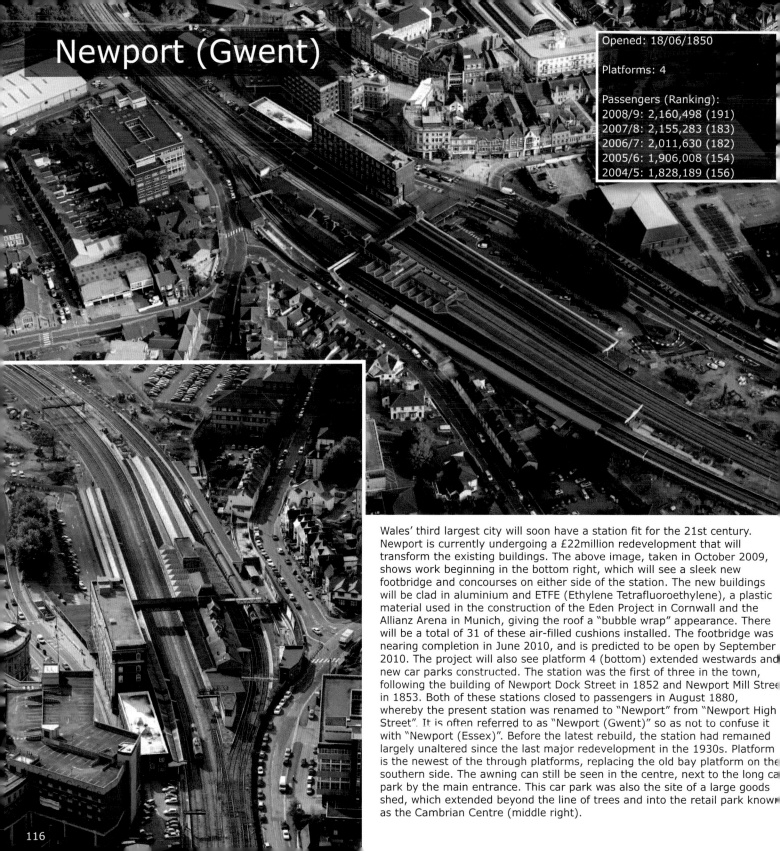

Newport (Gwent)

Opened: 18/06/1850

Platforms: 4

Passengers (Ranking):
2008/9: 2,160,498 (191)
2007/8: 2,155,283 (183)
2006/7: 2,011,630 (182)
2005/6: 1,906,008 (154)
2004/5: 1,828,189 (156)

Wales' third largest city will soon have a station fit for the 21st century. Newport is currently undergoing a £22million redevelopment that will transform the existing buildings. The above image, taken in October 2009, shows work beginning in the bottom right, which will see a sleek new footbridge and concourses on either side of the station. The new buildings will be clad in aluminium and ETFE (Ethylene Tetrafluoroethylene), a plastic material used in the construction of the Eden Project in Cornwall and the Allianz Arena in Munich, giving the roof a "bubble wrap" appearance. There will be a total of 31 of these air-filled cushions installed. The footbridge was nearing completion in June 2010, and is predicted to be open by September 2010. The project will also see platform 4 (bottom) extended westwards and new car parks constructed. The station was the first of three in the town, following the building of Newport Dock Street in 1852 and Newport Mill Street in 1853. Both of these stations closed to passengers in August 1880, whereby the present station was renamed to "Newport" from "Newport High Street". It is often referred to as "Newport (Gwent)" so as not to confuse it with "Newport (Essex)". Before the latest rebuild, the station had remained largely unaltered since the last major redevelopment in the 1930s. Platform is the newest of the through platforms, replacing the old bay platform on the southern side. The awning can still be seen in the centre, next to the long car park by the main entrance. This car park was also the site of a large goods shed, which extended beyond the line of trees and into the retail park known as the Cambrian Centre (middle right).

Northampton

Opened: 16/02/1859

Platforms: 6

Passengers (Ranking):
2008/9: 2,242,722 (176)
2007/8: 2,239,426 (177)
2006/7: 2,144,857 (170)
2005/6: 1,969,868 (146)
2004/5: 1,854,579 (155)

Formerly known as "Northampton Castle", the station originally opened in 1859 as the town's second station, after Northampton Bridge Street in May 1845. A third station, Northampton St John's Street, would open in June 1872. At the time it was opened Castle was only a small station, but that was to change when the town was directly connected to London via the opening of the Northampton Loop Line of the modern West Coast Main Line from 1879-1881. Northampton had originally been bypassed when the London & Birmingham Railway opened their completed line in 1838, but the new line enabled more trains to serve the town and therefore a bigger station was required, resulting in Castle being massively rebuilt. It was extended eastwards by the LNWR onto the site of the town's historic castle (c1084), from which it took its name. The LNWR bought the remaining foundations of the castle and built over them. Now all that remains is a section of a postern gate that

has been built into one of the boundary walls. The new station also featured a large 12-track goods shed on the eastern side, which is now the site of the large car park (right). The tracks that led into the shed remain as sidings, but perhaps not for long. In June 2010 it was announced that a redevelopment of the station would take place that would see a new 3-storey main building constructed, along with a large 6-storey car park on the site of the disused bay platform (centre, right). The sidings and the land to the north have been earmarked as the site of a large mixed-use development, comprising shops, offices and flats, with a date of 2014 estimated for the completion of the whole scheme. Since April 1966 the station has been known as "Northampton" following the closure of St John's Street (1939) and Bridge Street (1964).

Norwich Crown Point T.M.D.

The traction maintenance depot at Norwich is relatively new, having opened in October 1982. It was built at a cost of around £10 million and was designed to replace the old depot sited next to Norwich Thorpe Station, just a few hundred yards to the west. The original yards were constructed by the Norwich & Yarmouth Railway around 1844 at the same time as the station. These would be developed to include a large goods shed, bigger than the station itself, and many sidings. There was also a large locomotive shed manufacturing engines, located between the station and Crown Point, next to Norwich City's football ground. The Crown Point site was created with the opening of the loop line linking the Trowse Line (bottom left) with the Yarmouth Line (top right). For many years the land in between remained undeveloped, but several sidings had been built on the eastern side by the early 20th century, when it became known as Wensum Depot. These sidings are now the site of the main maintenance buildings, which is run by National Express East Anglia for the maintenance of diesel and intercity trains.

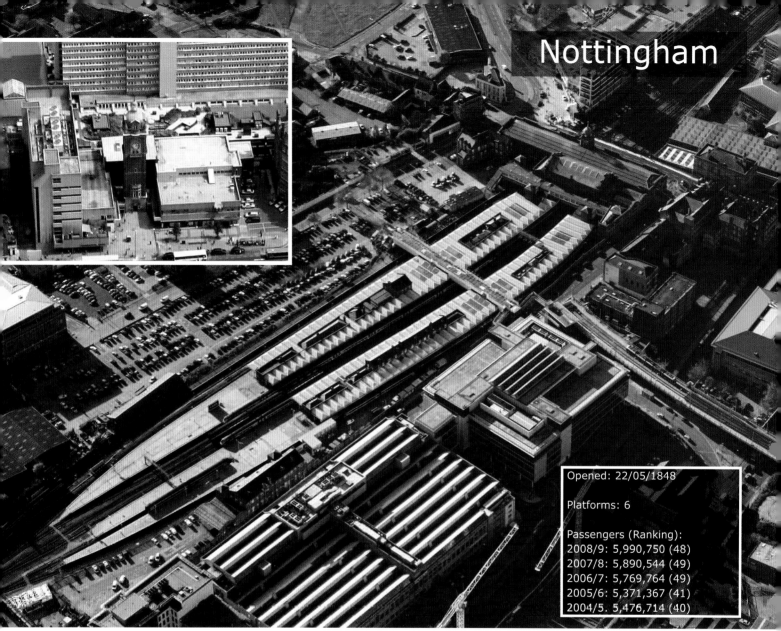

Nottingham

Opened: 22/05/1848

Platforms: 6

Passengers (Ranking):
2008/9: 5,990,750 (48)
2007/8: 5,890,544 (49)
2006/7: 5,769,764 (49)
2005/6: 5,371,367 (41)
2004/5: 5,476,714 (40)

reviously known as Nottingham Midland, this station was extensively ebuilt at the turn of the 20th century in order to compete with a rival tation opened in the north of the city centre. The line into Nottingham as opened by the Midland Counties Railway (later to become part of the lidland in 1844) on the route from Derby, which opened around May 839. The first station on the line was built just to the west of this image op right), and was known as Nottingham Carrington Street. When the ne to Lincoln was opened in 1846 this station would quickly prove to be nadequate, and so a new facility with 3 platforms was built slightly to ne east, on the opposite side of the street, with the entrances on tation Street (middle right). The old station site became a Midland oods yard and grain warehouse, and is now the site of Nottingham lagistrates' Court. The new station proved to be more successful, but hen the Great Central Railway opened Victoria station to the north in 900 it was soon overshadowed. The new station featured a 100ft clock ower, 12 platforms, and had sumptuous finishes throughout. Realising

something had to be done, in 1903 the Midland set about rebuilding their own station. They commissioned the same architect who had designed Victoria for their own plans, a man called Albert Edward Lambert. His design featured a terracotta and stone main building with huge porte-cochere (now directly facing onto Carrington Street), and the station was extended to 6 platforms, including one bay on the eastern side (bottom left). It was now more than a match for its rival, but the Midland were always left annoyed by the fact that the GCR line passed directly over their station on a 170ft bridge. This bridge is now demolished, but the approach viaduct has been redeveloped as part of the city's NET tram system (Nottingham Express Transit – right). A tram can be seen on the viaduct just leaving the new terminus block, which is linked to the railway station by a footbridge over Station Street. Victoria station was not to last, and was closed in September 1967. Today, only the clock tower remains as part of the Victoria Shopping Centre and flats complex (inset, top left).

Peterborough

Opened: 07/08/1850

Platforms: 5

Passengers (Ranking):
2008/9: 4,099,754 (77)
2007/8: 4,070,725 (73)
2006/7: 3,960,429 (76)
2005/6: 3,720,034 (65)
2004/5: 3,689,729 (67)

The magnificence of Peterborough's Norman cathedral is not matched by its station, which is now utilitarian at best. The first company to build a station in the city was the Eastern Counties Railway, who opened a station known as "Peterborough" to the south on the opposite bank of the River Nene, in June 1845. The Great Northern Railway were to follow the ECR into the city just a few years later. They opened their own loop line from Peterborough to Lincoln in October 1848, and at first used the ECR station. After attempting to purchase it in 1849, the decision was taken to build their own station, which would be on their new line to London King's Cross. Somewhat confusingly, this was also called "Peterborough". The ECR would become part of the Great Eastern Railway in 1862, and in 1923 both the GER and the GNR were merged into the new London & North Eastern Railway. This meant that both stations were owned by the same company, and so the names of the

stations has to be changed. The southern GER station became "Peterborough East" and the GNR station became "Peterborough North". When Peterborough East closed in June 1966, the remaining station reverted to "Peterborough". Although the modern station is in need of some attention, the GNR Hotel built opposite the booking hall is still standing (left). This opened in April 1852 at a cost of £2,500. The large L-shaped building to the right is a Royal Mail depot with its own footbridge for access to the platforms. Previously the site was home to large GNR engine and wagon works. To the north of the site there was also a large carriage shed on the western side of the tracks, which has since been demolished, but a second large carriage shed is still standing (top centre). The image shows that some of the tracks leading down to the main line are still in place, if now a little overgrown.

Plymouth

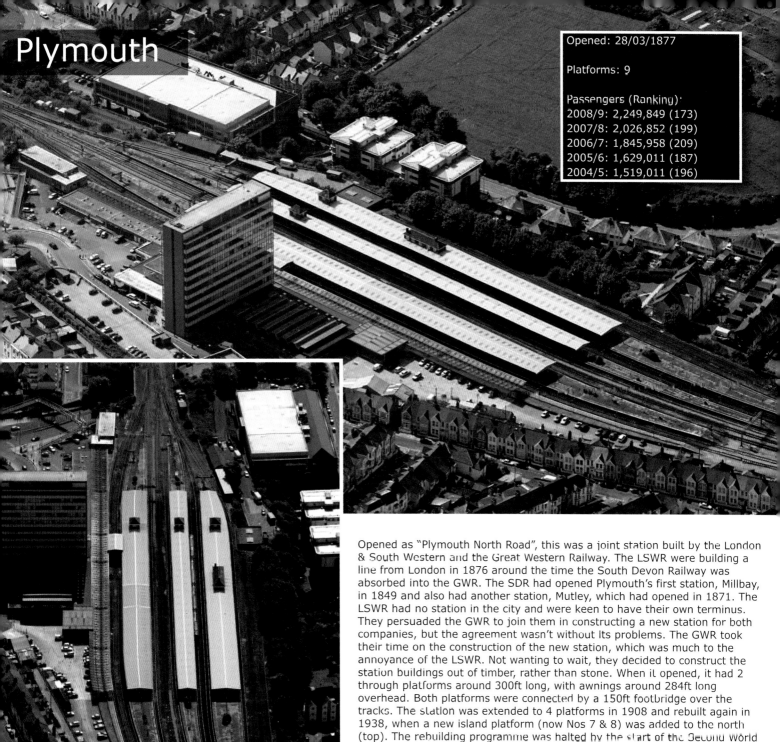

Opened: 28/03/1877

Platforms: 9

Passengers (Ranking):
2008/9: 2,249,849 (173)
2007/8: 2,026,852 (199)
2006/7: 1,845,958 (209)
2005/6: 1,629,011 (187)
2004/5: 1,519,011 (196)

Opened as "Plymouth North Road", this was a joint station built by the London & South Western and the Great Western Railway. The LSWR were building a line from London in 1876 around the time the South Devon Railway was absorbed into the GWR. The SDR had opened Plymouth's first station, Millbay, in 1849 and also had another station, Mutley, which had opened in 1871. The LSWR had no station in the city and were keen to have their own terminus. They persuaded the GWR to join them in constructing a new station for both companies, but the agreement wasn't without its problems. The GWR took their time on the construction of the new station, which was much to the annoyance of the LSWR. Not wanting to wait, they decided to construct the station buildings out of timber, rather than stone. When it opened, it had 2 through platforms around 300ft long, with awnings around 284ft long overhead. Both platforms were connected by a 150ft footbridge over the tracks. The station was extended to 4 platforms in 1908 and rebuilt again in 1938, when a new island platform (now Nos 7 & 8) was added to the north (top). The rebuilding programme was halted by the start of the Second World War. Following a bombing raid in April 1941 that hit Millbay, North Road became the city's main station. It was renamed as "Plymouth" in September 1958 as part of a £1.5m redevelopment plan that had been approved in February 1956. These plans followed on from the previously unfinished scheme of 1938. The new plans included the building of the adjoining ten-storey office block known as Intercity House. It was opened by Dr Richard Beeching on March 26th 1962, along with the new main concourse.

Porthmadog Harbour

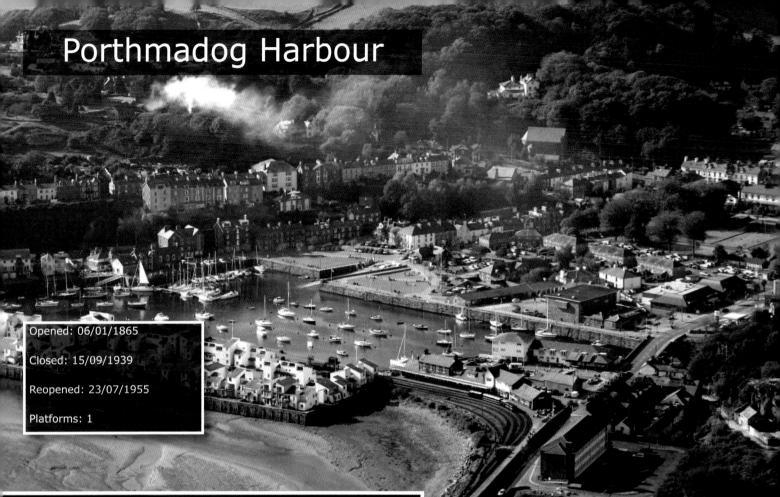

Opened: 06/01/1865

Closed: 15/09/1939

Reopened: 23/07/1955

Platforms: 1

The picturesque Harbour Station is home to the terminus of the Ffestiniog Railway. The railway was opened in April 1836 between Porthmadog and Blaenau Ffestiniog in the Snowdonian Mountains. The railway was set up to transport slate from the quarries high in the hills to the port below, where several slate wharves were built either side of the harbour by the station. The railway was built using a narrow gauge of 1ft 11 ½in based on that used in the quarries, and was powered by two different means. On the way down from the mines, gravity took the laden wagons down the 1:80 gradient 710ft high in the hills, for the full distance of 13 miles and 1,100 yards. On the way back, horses pulled the empty wagons back to the top. Steam engines on such a narrow gauge had been outlawed as unworkable, and it wasn't until 1863 that the first locos were allowed to operate on the route. In 1864 permission was granted to start running passenger services, and these commenced a year later - the first on a narrow gauge in Britain. The station is situated at the western end of the "Cob", a raised 1 mile embankment built from 1808-1811 by the tidal Afon Glaslyn River. The embankment is the only route to the station, providing spectacular views for its patrons. The station closed to passengers on September 15th 1939 following the declaration of war. It would reopen for slate mining for just one year after the war, before finally being closed on August 1st 1946. The closure wasn't to last long, however, as the railway was saved by a local group who set up the Ffestiniog Railway Trust. The line reopened in 1955 and is now a hugely popular tourist attraction.

Portsmouth & Southsea

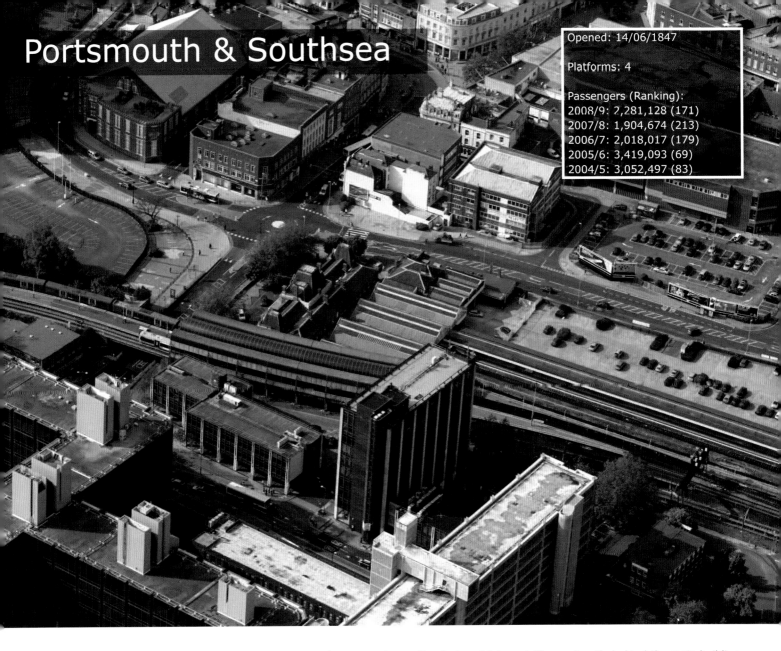

Opened: 14/06/1847

Platforms: 4

Passengers (Ranking):
2008/9: 2,281,128 (171)
2007/8: 1,904,674 (213)
2006/7: 2,018,017 (179)
2005/6: 3,419,093 (69)
2004/5: 3,052,497 (83)

e main station in Portsmouth has two distinctive sections. At the top, can see the site of the original terminus, and below we can see the gh level through platforms that were added in 1876. The station was st opened in 1847 as a joint station for the London, Brighton & South ast Railway, and the London & South Western. This was the terminus their route from Brighton via Chichester. The station was later linked the dockyards in the 1850s by a branch line that followed the course Unicorn Road along the edges of Victoria Park (top left). The line was sed in 1977. The present station buildings opened in 1866 when the ation was rebuilt. The main building features a large concourse and oking hall, and is resplendent in terracotta brick and yellow ndstone. Since 1999 it has been Grade II listed. To the rear we can e the glazed ridge and furrow roof and a large car park. When rebuilt

the station featured 3 bay platforms directly behind the main building, and this was extended by the addition of a further island to the north (top) around the turn of the 20th century. Today there are only 2 bays remaining. The next major work was the extension of the line to Portsmouth Harbour in 1876, following which the station became known as "Portsmouth Town". An additional long island platform was built on the south side for two new through lines. This section of track had to be elevated in order for then line to pass over Commercial Road (left). The high level platforms were crowned by the addition of a distinctive 3-arched glazed roof. Just to the south of this roof was the site of a large goods shed that opened around the same time of the station. The shed suffered bomb damage during the war and was no longer standing by 1951. The station has had its current name since 1925.

Portsmouth Harbour

Opened: 02/10/1876

Platforms: 5

Passengers (Ranking):
2008/9: 1,826,011 (228)
2007/8: 1,642,787 (251)
2006/7: 1,391,084 (282)
2005/6:   429,945 (615)
2004/5:   619,619 (458)

The harbour station opened as part of the London, Brighton & South Coast Railway, and the London & South Western Railway's new Portsmouth Waterside Extension in 1876. This allowed direct access to the coast and to the city's dockyards. The first station was a simple affair, and featured only two platforms on the northern side (top) of the present station. There was also a branch crossing the water over to the South Railway Jetty on Watering Island (top centre). By 1909 the station had been extended southwards to make a total of 5 platforms. This is the layout that exists today, although platform 2 is currently not in use. The station played a huge role in World War II with the mobilisation of troops and equipment for the D-Day landings on June 6th 1944, and the station suffered damage during several air raids in the years of conflict prior to this. Today, the station is flanked by icons of the city's past and present. At the top can be seen HMS warrior. The Royal Navy's flagship of 1860 and their first iron-hulled ship, it combined steam power with sail and was the fastest ship of the fleet. It is now a museum ship. On the left can be seen the 558ft Spinnaker Tower, an observation tower opened in 2005 offering views across the entire city and beyond. Passenger numbers for Portsmouth Harbour Station have risen dramatically in recent years. This can be partly attributed to the presence of the adjacent Gunwharf Quays shopping centre and leisure complex (bottom), which is a popular attraction.

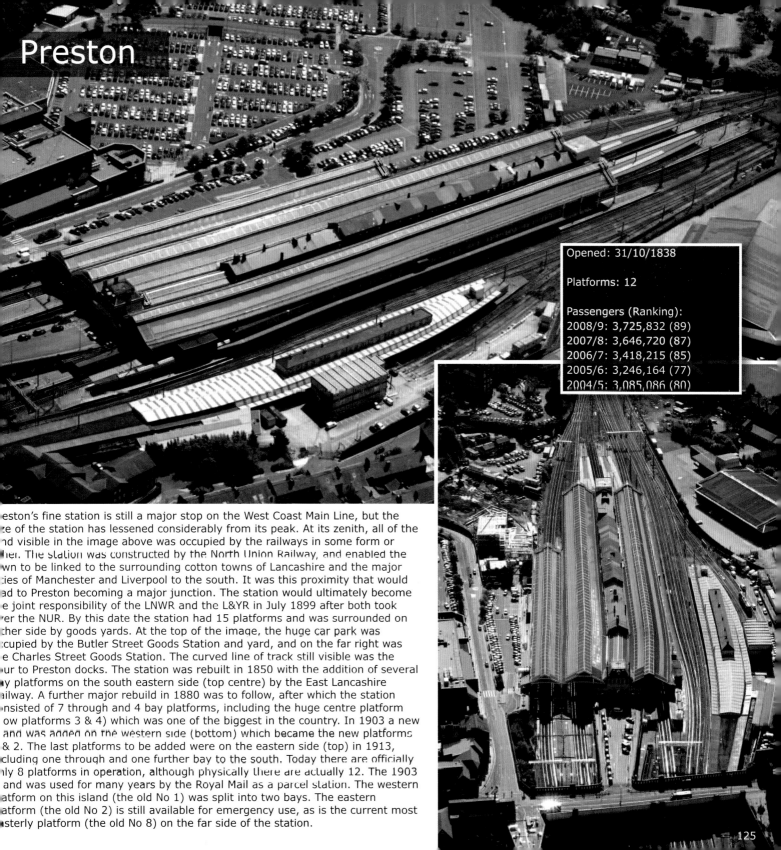

Preston

Opened: 31/10/1838

Platforms: 12

Passengers (Ranking):
2008/9: 3,725,832 (89)
2007/8: 3,646,720 (87)
2006/7: 3,418,215 (85)
2005/6: 3,246,164 (77)
2004/5: 3,085,086 (80)

eston's fine station is still a major stop on the West Coast Main Line, but the
ze of the station has lessened considerably from its peak. At its zenith, all of the
nd visible in the image above was occupied by the railways in some form or
her. The station was constructed by the North Union Railway, and enabled the
wn to be linked to the surrounding cotton towns of Lancashire and the major
ties of Manchester and Liverpool to the south. It was this proximity that would
ad to Preston becoming a major junction. The station would ultimately become
e joint responsibility of the LNWR and the L&YR in July 1899 after both took
er the NUR. By this date the station had 15 platforms and was surrounded on
ther side by goods yards. At the top of the image, the huge car park was
ccupied by the Butler Street Goods Station and yard, and on the far right was
e Charles Street Goods Station. The curved line of track still visible was the
ur to Preston docks. The station was rebuilt in 1850 with the addition of several
y platforms on the south eastern side (top centre) by the East Lancashire
ailway. A further major rebuild in 1880 was to follow, after which the station
nsisted of 7 through and 4 bay platforms, including the huge centre platform
ow platforms 3 & 4) which was one of the biggest in the country. In 1903 a new
and was added on the western side (bottom) which became the new platforms
& 2. The last platforms to be added were on the eastern side (top) in 1913,
cluding one through and one further bay to the south. Today there are officially
ly 8 platforms in operation, although physically there are actually 12. The 1903
and was used for many years by the Royal Mail as a parcel station. The western
atform on this island (the old No 1) was split into two bays. The eastern
atform (the old No 2) is still available for emergency use, as is the current most
sterly platform (the old No 8) on the far side of the station.

125

Reading

Opened: 30/03/1840

Platforms: 12

Passengers (Ranking):
2008/9: 14,384,236 (23)
2007/8: 14,549,487 (21)
2006/7: 14,367,752 (19)
2005/6: 13,570,560 (18)
2004/5: 13,297,027 (18)

Reading is one of the most important and busiest stations in the south and was the original terminus of the first section of the Great Western Railway in 1840. The original station, designed by Brunel, received a new main building around 1865. The building (centre), features a central clock tower, has Bath stone dressings and is Grade II listed. The whole site was a major hub for the GWR. The land to the north (bottom) was a GWR works and there were depots and goods sheds at either end of the station. In 1849 a second station was built right next door on the southern side. This was a terminus station constructed by the Reading, Guildford & Redhill Railway. For much of its life it was known as "Reading South" or "Reading Southern", and at its biggest it had 4 bay platforms. From 1846 it was leased by the SER, who absorbed the RG&RR in 1852. It remained a separate station until March 1965, but was to close to passengers in September of that year.

It remained as a goods station for 5 years before being redeveloped in 1989 as a large new concourse for the main station (centre left). This featured a large new footbridge connecting it to both the platforms and a new multi storey car park on the old works site (bottom left). Despite having 12 platforms, the station only has 4 through platforms and is a notorious bottleneck. In mid 2010 plans were announced by Network Rail for a £400m redevelopment of the station that would see 5 new platforms built on the north side, along with a new connecting footbridge and new entrances and concourses on both the north and the south sides. There will also be new freight lines. Preparatory works have already started, and total completion of the project is hoped for 2016. The work should enable the capacity of the station to reach 35 million passengers per year.

This is one of the smallest stations in the UK, but it is also one of the most historic and most scenic. Ribblehead station was opened by the Midland Railway as part of the Settle to Carlisle Railway, when the company were seeking an alternative route to Scotland via Yorkshire and the East Midlands. Over 6,000 navies worked on its construction from 1869-1875, making it the last manually built railway in Britain. The station is at the southern end of the magnificent Ribblehead Viaduct (also known as the Batty Moss Railway Viaduct). Designed by the engineer John Crossley, the viaduct is 1,320ft long (¼ of a mile) and 104 ft high. It features 24 segmental arches amongst its curved length and was built between 1870 and 1874. It is now Grade II* listed and a Scheduled Ancient Monument. The station closed in May 1970 but was to reopen in 1986, albeit with only one platform. The original down platform had been demolished, but a replacement was opened in March 1993 further down the line. In the image we can see the main station building with the original Up platform. The station is now leased by the Settle & Carlisle Railway Trust. After being restored the building now includes a shop and a visitor centre with details of the line's history.

Opened: 01/05/1876

(Closed: 04/051970;
Reopened: 14/07/1986)

Platforms: 2

Passengers (Ranking):
2008/9: 16,940 (2159)
2007/8: 14,046 (2172)
2006/7: 15,265 (2135)
2005/6: 14,870 (2104)
2004/5: 15,371 (2083)

Romford

Romford is a busy commuter station to the north east of London. Historically in Essex and now officially part of Greater London in the Borough of Havering, the town grew rapidly following the arrival of the railway in 1839. The line into Romford was built by the Eastern Counties Railway from a terminus at Devonshire Street Station in Mile End, east London. This was only a temporary terminus, and it closed a year later when Bishopsgate Station was opened in Shoreditch. This route would later become an integral part of the Great Eastern Mainline from Liverpool Street to Norwich, when the ECR became part of the GER in 1862.

The station originally had 2 through platforms on the south side (right), but this was extended in the 1920s to 4 with the creation of a new island platform. At first glance there only appears to be these 4 platforms, but there are actually 5. The fifth is a bay platform visible at the top centre of the photograph. This was an entirely separate station opened by the London, Tilbury & Southend Railway on June 7th 1893. Originally this station had two platforms with the second on the north side, and was part of the single line branch to Grays via Upminster. The original station building is still standing, and can be seen by the side of the tracks. It is the square building with the bright white face immediately to the right of the rail bridge. The station officially closed on April 4th 1932 when it was integrated into the main Romford station.

A connecting footbridge was built on the rail bridge directly over South Street below, to allow passengers to connect between the two stations. The small bus depot on the right was also the site of a goods station built at the lower level. It extended as far as South Street towards the top of the picture, and was approached from a spur at the western end (bottom right).

Opened: 20/06/1839

Platforms: 5

Passengers (Ranking):
2008/9: 7,310,172 (40)
2007/8: 8,372,672 (33)
2006/7: 7,363,378 (31)
2005/6: 4,823,860 (48)
2004/5: 5,118,900 (44)

St Helens Central

Helens' recently opened new entrance building has helped to
nsform what had become a tired and fairly run down station. The new
ding features a double height waiting room, ticket office, booking
and toilets, along with a new pedestrian footbridge and first floor
. Designed by SBS Architects, the new building opened in
tember 2007 at a cost of £6.2 million. The station was built to
lace the town's third station situated just to the north on the
osite side of the road bridge (top right). This had opened on
ruary 1st 1858, but never resembled anything more than a
porary station. It was built by the St Helens Railway Company, but
1864 this had become part of the London & North Western Railway,
they opened the present station on a new line to Huyton on the
e day that the old station closed. The site of the old station went on
to be developed as a considerable
goods yard. The new station was
known as "St Helens" until March
1949 when it was renamed "St
Helens Shaw Street". At its largest it featured two large island platforms
offering 3 through rails and 3 small bays at the southern side. Each
island was covered by an imposing pitched roof that covered the width
of the platforms, and the facing tracks. The roofs were demolished in
the early 1960s. The original eastern island is now all that remains (the
pale concrete on the right). This is now fenced off and a new platform
has been added along its side. One of the old bay platforms is still
visible at the southern end (bottom left). Since May 1987 the station
has been known as "St Helens Central".

Located just a few hundred yards south west of Manchester Victoria and Exchange, Salford Central predated them both, opening as the eastern terminus of the Manchester & Bolton Railway on the same day as Bolton Trinity Street in 1838. It was physically connected to Victoria when that station opened in 1844, with the rail line being carried high above the street on a series of viaducts and bridges (top left).

The city of Salford is always somewhat overshadowed by its larger neighbour, and the same could be said for its main railway station, which despite recent investment is still lagging far behind the rebuilt Piccadilly and other stations similar in size to itself. Salford Central currently only has two operational platforms on the northern side (left). Platforms 3 & 4 (centre) no longer have any track, and the Chat Moss Lines (right) which form part of the route to Liverpool, don't have any platforms. In September 2008 Network Rail released details of the possibility of adding platforms to these lines at some point in the future, but as yet no final decision on the idea has been made.

What the station does have is an excellent new glazed entrance and booking hall at street level, below the New Bailey Street bridge (centre). This was built as part of a £5 million upgrade that opened in February 2008. Due to its proximity to Manchester City Centre, the station could be used as another gateway point to its neighbour, but passenger numbers remain relatively low. Of interest in the image are the car parks on the right hand side. This was the site of Salford Goods Station, which stretched for several hundred yards westwards along the banks of the River Irwell, on what is now Man Central Trading Estate. Much of this site is currently awaiting redevelopment.

Opened: 28/05/1838

Platforms: 4 (2 in use)

Passengers (Ranking):
2008/9: 221,922 (1178)
2007/8: 124,720 (1383)
2006/7: 118,807 (1364)
2005/6: 116,794 (1316)
2004/5: 102,154 (1352)

Salisbury

Opened: 02/05/1859

Platforms: 6

Passengers (Ranking):
2008/9: 1,757,216 (237)
2007/8: 1,681,413 (247)
2006/7: 1,620,677 (236)
2005/6: 1,603,255 (192)
2004/5: 1,560,337 (190)

existing station here was actually the third to be built in the city. It opened by the Salisbury and Yeovil Railway on a line connecting the don & South Western Railway's tracks in Devon and Cornwall to its n networks around London. The LSWR operated the new line and nally bought the S&YR in 1878. The LSWR had opened the first ion in Salisbury in 1847, which was known as Milford Station. The nd station was a GWR terminus that was built on a site just north of rchfield Road (top left). This was a modest terminus utilising the R broad gauge, on the Wiltshire, Somerset & Weymouth Railway. It ned on June 30th 1856 with two platforms and two further central ks under a wooden shed. It is now the site of Salisbury Traction ntenance Depot (bottom right). The old station buildings designed by nbard Kingdom Brunel still stand, although not in picture. Since

October 1972 they have been Grade II listed. This station was soon overshadowed by the new LSWR station, which was built on the remaining land between Churchfield Road and the GWR terminus. Although run by different companies, the two stations were connected by a footbridge to enable passengers to move freely between them. This footbridge was closed in 1956. The LSWR station was considerably rebuilt around 1902, increasing the total number of platforms to 6 with 2 bays either end of the current platform 4 (left). The 1902 station building has been Grade II listed since October 2008. The GWR station finally closed on September 12th 1932 when the site became a goods depot. The current T.M.D. was opened in 1992 for South West Trains. It features 5 sidings and a large shed, just in shot on the right.

Saltash - The Royal Albert Bridge

One of Isambard Kingdom Brunel's masterpieces, the Royal Albert Bridge spans the River Tamar betw
Devon and Cornwall at Saltash. It was built as part of the Cornwall Railway that took the line from
Plymouth to Falmouth. The original plans in 1845 had proposed that trains could cross the Tamar via
ferry at Torpoint, but this was rejected by Parliament and Brunel took over the scheme in 1846. His p
was to build a huge wrought-iron bridge spanning the river at its narrowest point (1,100ft). Construc
started in 1854 and was to take over 5 years to complete. The main features of the bridge are the tw
"Bow String" sections directly above the river, each with a span of 455ft. At its highest point the brid
reaches 172 feet and has a clearance below of exactly 100ft. Its overall length, including the sections
over land, is 2187 ½ft. It was completed in April 1859, but the official ceremony did not take place
May 2nd when it was declared open by Prince Albert. Two days later the line, and the small Saltash
station on the western side of the bridge, was opened. Brunel did not attend the opening due to illne
and he would die later that year on September 5th. To mark his memory and his achievements, Brur
name was added at either end of the bridge (small image, left). Celebrations were held on the 100th
150th anniversaries of the bridge, including in 2009 when a guided walk was held along its full length
1961 the bridge received a new companion when the adjacent Tamar Bridge was opened for road tra

Selby

Opened: 18/09/1834

Platforms: 3

Passengers (Ranking):
2008/9: 475,020 (752)
2007/8: 472,699 (693)
2006/7: 442,689 (685)
2005/6: 406,344 (640)
2004/5: 394,559 (637)

The historic station at Selby, the first passenger station in Yorkshire, still stands alongside its successor. The large shed on the right hand side was the original terminus of the Leeds & Selby Railway that opened in 1834. The line was built as direct competition to the Aire & Calder Navigation, which ran from Knottingley to Goole via Leeds. At Selby, goods from Leeds could be transported to the major centres of York and Hull, as well as to the continent, via the River Ouse (right), which leads directly into the Humber and the North Sea. The shed was altered by a total of 6 tracks, four of which were used for goods. There were also a large number of external sidings on the eastern side (bottom). The remains of some of these tracks can still be seen in the receding yard (centre) in the photograph. The station was converted to goods use in 1841 when a new through station was built alongside it.

This was constructed by the Hull & Selby Railway, extending the existing line to the port at Hull via a swing bridge over the Ouse. The L&SR line was connected to York via the completion of the York & North Midland Railway in 1840, which would become part of the NER in 1854. The NER rebuilt Selby station into the layout that exists today. It reopened on January 2nd 1871 with two through platforms and two bay platforms on both the Up and Down side. Only one of these bays is still in operation, and the bay on the western side has since been filled in and is now used as a car park. Following being taken over by the NER, the station became an important stop on the East Coast Main Line, but the limitations imposed by the swing bridge meant that the route was diverted away from the town in 1983. Both the original terminus building and the current Selby station are Grade II listed.

Sheffield

Opened: 01/02/1870

Platforms: 9

Passengers (Ranking):
2008/9: 7,334,436 (39)
2007/8: 5,848,050 (50)
2006/7: 5,589,901 (52)
2005/6: 5,167,429 (42)
2004/5: 5,000,841 (46)

Sheffield remains one of the busiest stations in the north of England and has seen considerable growth in usage in recent years. The station occupies a large site to the east of the city centre and now has an adjoining Sheffield Supertram station on the eastern side (right). A tram can be seen heading for the station in the lower middle of the image. The station opened relatively late after the railway boom and was not the city's first. That honour went to the Sheffield & Rotherham Railway's Wicker Station to the north of the city centre. This opened in October 1838 in response to George Stephenson's refusal to route his North Midland Railway through the city, instead bypassing it to the east to avoid building large and expensive tunnels through the hilly landscape. The present station was opened by the Midland Railway in 1870. They had acquired the S&RR in July 1845 (although they had been running the line since the previous year) and built the new station on a new connecting route to Chesterfield. The original station building are still standing, but now occupy part of the large island platform in the middle. This was a consequence of a substantial rebuilding programme undertaken by Charles Trubshaw in 1905, which extended the station to the west. The new station frontage included a huge 12-bay porte-cochere and glazed ridge & furrow roof, now Grade II listed The land immediately in front of the entrance was home to the Pond Street Goods Station, which also opened in 1870. This closed in October 1961 and in 1965 Sheaf House, a nine-storey office block for British Rail, opened on the site along with Dyson House, a large building for Sheffield Hallam University. Both were demolished in 200! and 2006 to make way for the new Sheaf Square public realm by the main entrance, which has helped to improve both the appearance of and the approach to the station.

National Railway Museum - Shildon

hildon's history will forever be associated with the railways as it was he terminus of the original Stockton & Darlington Railway in 1825. The hildon branch of the line was built to transport coal from the extensive ollieries around the town to the docks at Stockton. Because of this, hildon Railway Works was to open in the town on September 27th 825. The area around the original station is now home to the Shildon rm of the National Railway Museum, known as "Shildon Locomotion useum". The museum is based around several historic buildings along he line of the railway. On the far east of the site is the main exhibition uilding (above), where the museum houses some of its important olling stock and other historic items associated with Shildon and the ailways, including an original Advanced Passenger Train Experimental APT-E). This is also the home of the conservation workshop, where

visitors can see engines and artefacts being restored. Other buildings include the former Goods Shed, the old Parcel Office, Coal Drops, and Timothy Hackworth's house. Hackworth was the chief locomotive superintendent at the works, a position he held until May 1840. Whilst in the job he began to build his own locomotives (the first was the "Royal George"), which would ultimately lead to the beginning of locomotive and wagon manufacturing at the site. Hackworth even entered his own engine into the Rainhill Trials in 1829, called "Sans Pareil" ("Without Equal", in English). The loco didn't win, but it impressed enough to serve on the Liverpool & Manchester Railway for two years. There is now a 1980 replica of the engine in the Collections building, and the remains of the original are housed in the Welcome building.

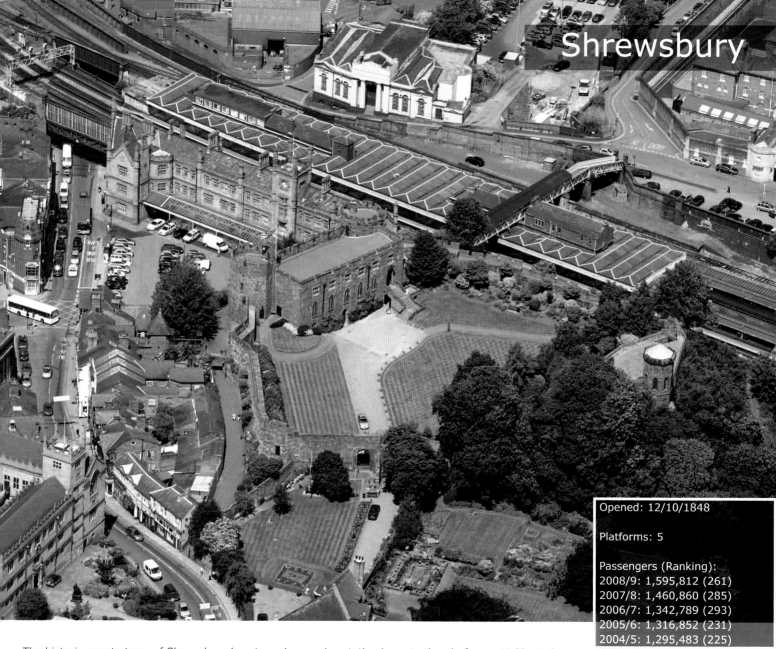

Opened: 12/10/1848

Platforms: 5

Passengers (Ranking):
2008/9: 1,595,812 (261)
2007/8: 1,460,860 (285)
2006/7: 1,342,789 (293)
2005/6: 1,316,852 (231)
2004/5: 1,295,483 (225)

The historic county town of Shrewsbury boasts an impressive station in an impressive location. The station is situated alongside the 11th century castle and is approached over the River Severn from the south. The station was built by four companies as a joint station, all of whom had interest in building lines to or through the town. These were the Shrewsbury & Chester Railway, the Shrewsbury & Birmingham Railway, the Shrewsbury & Hereford Railway and the Shropshire Union Railways & Canal Company. It would later be operated jointly by the GWR and the LNWR. The companies commissioned architect Thomas Penson to design the building for them, and he came up with an elaborate Tudor-gothic style façade that is now Grade II listed. The station was originally only two storeys tall, but rebuilding works added an extra floor below the existing structure in 1901, along with an access tunnel to the platforms. Unlike today, the station was also entirely covered by a large iron roof. The north end of the roof survived until 1924, whilst the southern end was dismantled in the 1960s. Shrewsbury currently has five operational platforms, but there are two bays at the southern end that have had their track removed. The station is also famous for its signal box. Known as the Severn Bridge Junction Signal Box, it is the largest surviving mechanical signal box in the UK, and possibly the world, with a total of 180 levers. Built by the LNWR, it opened in 1904 at the southern end of the station on the opposite side of the Severn, in between the branch lines to Wolverhampton and Ludlow.

Southampton Terminus (site of)

Opened: 11/05/1840

Closed: 05/09/1966

Platforms: 6

Southampton Terminus Station closed in 1966 but the remaining structures are still instantly recognisable as a railway station. The ridge and furrow canopy added around 1924 and the original station building on the right are still extant, although there are now no remains of the platforms. This section is now used as a car park, and has been for many years. The old goods shed that was built in the 1840s is still standing, just out of shot in the bottom left, and is now a covered car park for the flats shown here. The old 1860s station hotel (Originally "The Imperial Hotel", and later renamed "The South Western") still stands at the head of the station, but it has now been converted into flats. Terminus Station was built by the London & Southampton railway, with work starting in 1834. By the time the station was ready the L&SR had been renamed as the London & South Western Railway, reflecting their desires to expand into a greater area. The station opened in 1840 but it was actually ready in June 1839. It could not open at that time as

the line was still incomplete between Winchester and Basingstoke. The main station building has an impressive Italianate façade designed by Sir William Tite, and is Grade II* listed. The main purpose of the line to the city was to take advantage of its dockyards and ferry services, allowing passengers from London to go all of the way to the coast. After the station opened the docks developed rapidly and were soon covered in dozens of large warehouses holding grains, timber and other goods. So prevalent were they, that in 1858 the station was renamed as "Southampton Docks" from "Southampton". Further name changes would see it rebranded as "Southampton Town & Docks" in 1896, "Southampton Town (For Docks)" in 1912, and finally to "Southampton Terminus" in 1923. Somewhat ironically, Southampton City Council has plans to build a small station on the remaining freight lines that still lead to the docks. This will be located on the grassed area on the lower left, up to where the tracks meet the main road.

Southport

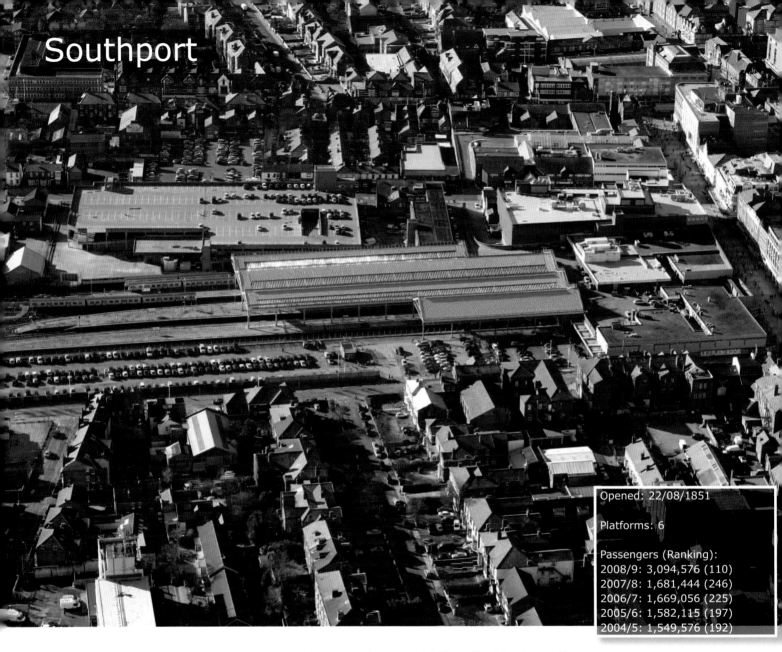

Southport station opened as Chapel Street Station on the Liverpool, Crosby & Southport Railway in 1851. The line was actually opened on July 24th 1848 between Liverpool Waterloo and a temporary terminus at Southport called Eastbank Street. This station closed on the day that Chapel Street opened, but the ticket office and Station Master's house are still in place by the side of the railway. They are situated next to a level crossing on Portland Street, some 300 yards down the track on the Merseyrail Northern Line. Southport is the northern terminus of the Merseyrail system, which is centred on Liverpool. In the image we can see 3 Merseyrail Class 507 EMUs in their familiar yellow livery, which operate out of platforms 1-3. The station was taken over by the Lancashire & Yorkshire Railway in July 1897, which led to some

rebuilding. The West Lancashire Railway had opened a station a few streets away to the east in 1882, called Southport Central. The WLR was also absorbed by the L&YR, and they decided to concentrate all services on Chapel Street. This resulted in the closure of the WLR station in May 1901, along with reworking of the tracks to allow all services to enter Chapel Street. Southport Central was then used as a goods yard until the 1970s. The station was greatly expanded on the northern side to include two additional islands, taking the total number of platforms to 11. These platforms have since been demolished and the land is now used as a car park (lower middle). The original 3 islands remain, but the old station concourse has been replaced by retail units that now front onto Chapel Street (far right).

Stafford

Opened: 04/07/1837

Platforms: 6

Passengers (Ranking):
2008/9: 1,493,852 (294)
2007/8: 1,250,054 (333)
2006/7: 1,155,373 (338)
2005/6: 1,072,661 (282)
2004/5: 1,016,196 (291)

The small county town of Stafford has a very large station, far bigger than its size warrants. This is due to its importance as a major junction on the West Coast Main Line. To the south of the station, the lines from Rugby (The Trent Valley Line) and the line via Birmingham (The Rugby, Birmingham & Stafford Line) merge, making the station more important than it otherwise would have been. The present station dates from a rebuild in 1962 that coincided with the electrification of the WCML. The result is a brutalist reinforced concrete structure that is efficient, if not easy on the eye. The five through platforms are linked by a large footbridge with glazed sides. This allows excellent views down on to the tracks below, making the station a favourite with train enthusiasts. The footbridge is unusual in that there are seating areas along its length to take advantage of the views. The footbridge directly connects with the Royal Mail sorting depot on the western side (top), where there is a special mail-only platform with its own roof which runs for the length of the station. The small bay platform (No 2, bottom left) is now rarely used for passenger services. The original station was constructed by George Stephenson's and Joseph Locke's Grand Junction Railway in 1837. The route extends the line from Birmingham to Warrington, and from here it would eventually reach the Liverpool & Manchester Railway at Newton Junction, near Newton-le-Willows. The station was to prove so busy that two quick rebuilds took place, one in 1844 (a two storey building in Tudor style) and a third in 1862 by the London & North Western, who had taken over the GJR in 1846. The LNWR also built a substantial railway hotel, known as the North Western Hotel, on the site of the large white buildings (bottom right) around 1866. It lasted until 1972 when it was demolished.

Stockport

Stockport viaduct is a spectacular feat of Victorian engineering that dominates the surrounding town centre and makes the West Coast Main Line possible. Stockport town centre is built in the valley of the River Mersey (centre, which starts in the town), and this valley presented the biggest obstacle to construction on the Manchester & Birmingham Railway. Designed by John Lowe and built by the engineer George Watson Buck, the viaduct is an enormous 1786ft long and 111 feet high. It is built almost entirely of ordinary household bricks. A total of 11 million were used in its construction, making it the largest brick-built structure in Western Europe. Work started with the laying of the foundation stone on June 4th 1839 and finished on December 21st 1840. The total cost was £70,000. Before the viaduct opened, trains from Manchester stopped at the former Heaton Norris station to the north of the valley (left), on the first section of the line. When it opened, the route to Birmingham opened with it, signalling a boom in the town's already huge cotton and hat making industries. The viaduct was extended on the eastern side to four tracks between 1887 and 1889, enabling a greater number of services to cross the divide. In total, there are 27 arches, including 22 large and 5 small, and it is Grade II* listed. In 1989 the viaduct was cleaned for the first time at a cost of £3million, removing 150 years of grime that had built up from the town's factories. It was also floodlit, and is now a major landmark on the M60 Motorway. The viaduct's arches are just big enough to carry the separate lanes of the motorway, which was opened in 1982.

Stockport Station (opposite page, bottom) is a major stop on the West Coast Main Line, being the last port of call before Manchester 7 miles to the north. It was opened by the Manchester & Birmingham Railway in 1843 but later came under the control of the LNWR and then the London, Midland & Scottish Railway. In 1923 the LMS renamed it as "Stockport Edgeley" to distinguish it from the Cheshire Lines Committee's Stockport Tiviot Dale Station (1865-1967) to the north east of the town centre (the site of the station is visible in the top left of the main image, under the motorway). Today the station is often referred to as "Edgeley", the inner suburb to the immediate west, but it is officially "Stockport". At its largest the station had 9 platforms on the two existing wide islands, including 5 bays. Only one of these bays now remains in use, but the roof on the eastern island (top) still has the cuttings designed to allow the trains into the platforms. The bays have been filled in, with the exception of a section of the bay at the south of the western platform (bottom), which is used as a small garden. The remaining operational bay (left) is used for some local services and for the famous Parliamentary service to Stalybridge, which runs just once a week. In September 2004 the station gained a new glazed double-height entrance and booking hall, along with a new platform (top). The platform did not open until March 2008 due to claims that it could not be connected to the old Victorian signal box that is still in operation (lower right, on the platform). This is Edgeley Junction No.1, which was added by the LNWR in 1884. The new platform was named "Platform 0", one of only a handful in the UK to bear this number. The considerable sidings on the western side are still used. These were once contained within a large carriage shed. On the eastern side the land now occupied by the large car park (right) was home to a goods shed and associated sidings, whilst the land with the large white buildings was the site of a large coal yard. This is now the Grand Central Leisure complex.

Swansea High Street

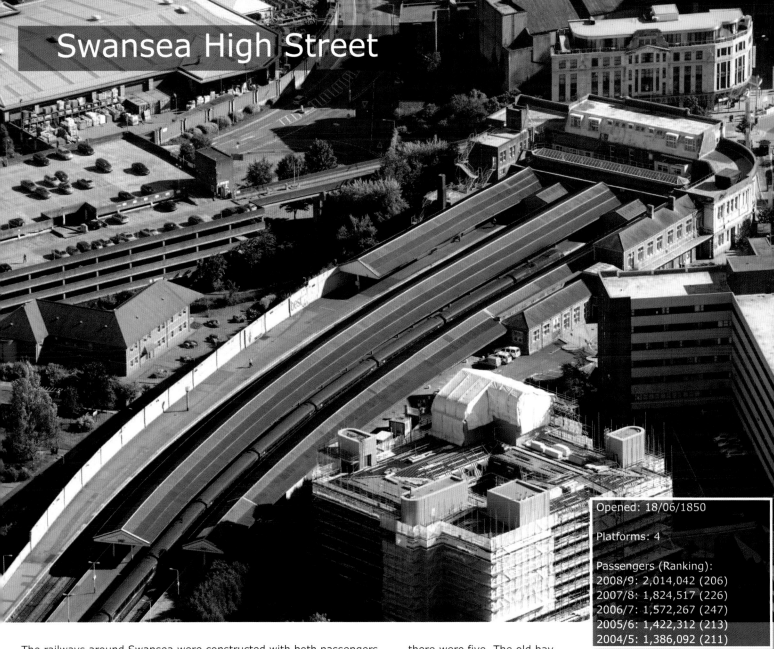

Opened: 18/06/1850

Platforms: 4

Passengers (Ranking):
2008/9: 2,014,042 (206)
2007/8: 1,824,517 (226)
2006/7: 1,572,267 (247)
2005/6: 1,422,312 (213)
2004/5: 1,386,092 (211)

The railways around Swansea were constructed with both passengers and coal in mind. The valleys of South Wales were a major source of coal, and good connections were required to transport it to the rest of the country. The South Wales Railway was set up for this purpose. Using the broad gauge system, the line took a branch from the Great Western Railway at Standish near Stroud, Gloucestershire. The line was partly funded by the GWR, and they eventually leased the line once it was completed. The section of track from Swansea to Chepstow was the first to be completed in 1850, which resulted in the opening of Swansea High Street station. The GWR would eventually absorb the SWR in 1862, but not before Brunel had linked the two via Chepstow Bridge in 1852, which was the prototype for his bridge at Saltash. The original High Street Station had only two platforms, but at its largest there were five. The old bay platform on the western side (right) has since been filled in, but the awnings remain as a reminder of its presence. The station is now a terminus but there was a connecting line through on the eastern side to the other major station in the city, Swansea Victoria, although through trains had to reverse to enter the platforms here. This line was lifted in November 1965. The station today is the western terminus for services from London Paddington and it is soon to get a revamp. In February 2010 plans were announced for a series of upgrades to the station, which were later confirmed in August. The station will get a new booking office, new shelters, and a much larger concourse. The rear wall of the concourse will be glazed to allow light inside from the platform area.

Swindon

Opened: July 1842

Platforms: 4

Passengers (Ranking):
2008/9. 2,905,266 (121)
2007/8: 2,758,891 (127)
2006/7: 2,515,492 (132)
2005/6: 2,340,952 (111)
2004/5: 2,257,719 (111)

indon played a huge role in the railway industry, being home to the
eat Western's main locomotive, wagon and carriage works. At it's
ak the works employed over 12,000 people and it covered an area of
se to 326 acres, just to the west of Swindon station. The works were
ed at Swindon as it was located close to the GWR's Cheltenham
anch junction and to the Wilts & Berks Canal. The chief engineer,
niel Gooch, recommended the location to Isambard Kingdom Brunel,
d after approval from the GWR board work commenced on the site in
oruary 1841. The facilities included all manner of engine sheds,
inting and lifting shops, carriage sheds and finishing sheds. There was
o a railway village built to house new workers coming into the town.
e works were to open on January 2nd 1843, by which time the station
s already open and operational, and known as "Swindon Junction".
e station had two large island platforms connected by an enclosed

footbridge. On each platform was a three-storey stone building in a
Georgian style. The platforms featured the world's first station
refreshment rooms, and as a means of making money each train visiting
Swindon would stop for at least ten minutes for a refreshment break.
Only one of the original islands now remains. The eastern island was
demolished in the 1970s and replaced by the large office block for
British Rail (the building still carries the BR insignia at the top). In 2003
a new facing platform (No. 4, with the grey flat roof) was opened here
along with waiting rooms to the rear. Swindon Works declined heavily
after World War II. Much of the site was closed in 1967 for
redevelopment, and the end came in 1986 when the last remaining
workshops closed. Most of the site had been completely redeveloped,
but many listed buildings remain, and there is now a GWR museum
known as "Steam", which is housed in some of the original workshops.

Opened: 30/07/1863

Platforms: 2

Passengers (Ranking):
2008/9: 92,892 (1595)
2007/8: 94,231 (1532)
2006/7: 84,598 (1538)
2005/6: 75,629 (1521)
2004/5: 76,695 (1498)

The delightful seaside town of Tenby, famed for its medieval town walls, is served by a small but functional station. The line into the town was built by the Pembroke & Tenby Railway Company, who gained parliamentary authority for the railway in 1859. There had been previous plans for a line to Pembroke dating back to 1844, but the permission for this line, closely associated to the GWR, had lapsed by the later date. Construction on the new line started almost immediately at a cost of £106,000, with the first section, from Tenby to Pembroke, opening at the end of July 1863. The last section, from Pembroke to Pembroke Dock, opened just over a year later on August 8th, taking the total route to 11 ¾ miles. The railway was eventually linked to the GWR at Whitland, Carmarthenshire, in September 1866. The P&TR had been built with standard gauge, meaning it could not be linked physically to

the GWR line, so there were adjoining stations constructed here, with the Pembroke line on the south side. The P&TR's chief engineer was S James Weeks Szlumper, who worked on parts of the London Underground, and he rebuilt Tenby station to the existing design following a locomotive crash. There are currently only two operational platforms, but the line of the old third platform can still be seen on the left. The original buildings on the western platform were replaced with the current awnings around 1856. At Tenby there was also a small goods depot, situated just to the left of this image, and an interesting viaduct just to the north (top left) with seven arches. The Pembroke & Tenby Railway was eventually leased to the GWR in 1896 following its conversion to standard gauge in 1892, and formally absorbed in 1897

Tonbridge

Opened: 26/05/1842

Platforms: 4

Passengers (Ranking):
2008/9: 4,211,562 (74)
2007/8: 4,314,602 (70)
2006/7: 4,115,454 (74)
2005/6: 3,931,393 (61)
2004/5: 3,810,457 (63)

espite only having a population of 30,000, Tonbridge Station has
corded passenger numbers of close to, or over, 4 million for the past
e years. This can be explained by its location within the London
mmuter belt, and also partly by its position on the line to the ports at
over and Folkestone. The station was built as the original terminus of
e South Eastern Railway, which gained its first Royal Ascent on June
st 1836 to build a line from London to Dover. Work did not start on
e line until November 1837 when the first tracks were laid at Reigate
d here at Tonbridge, or "Tunbridge", as the town was known until
70. Under the auspices of engineer William Cubitt, the line from
ndon Bridge to Tunbridge was completed on May 26th 1842. It was
ly the terminus for a short period, as the remainder of the line
ened to Ashford on December 1st, followed by Folkestone in June

1843 and finally Dover on
February 2nd 1844. The first
station was built of timber a few hundred yards to the east. It was
rebuilt at its present site in 1857, by which time it was known as
"Tunbridge Junction", so as not to confuse it with Tunbridge Wells (a
short 5-mile branch south to Tunbridge Wells opened in 1845). The
rebuild created a new entrance at street level (right). This was rebuilt in
1935 by the Southern Railway, along with improvements to the
platforms. The old bay platform on the southern side (bottom) was also
converted to a new through-line at this time. Following the change of
the town's name by the GPO, the station was renamed as "Tonbridge
Junction" in 1893, and again to "Tonbridge" in 1929.

Tunbridge Wells

The station at Royal Tunbridge Wells is tiny, but nonetheless very impressive. It was opened by the SER on their branch line to Hastings, which gained approval in 1845. The first section of the line was completed the same year, and terminated at a temporary station on the town's outskirts on September 20th. The permanent station did not open until the following year after the lengthy construction of the 823-yard long Wells Tunnel. The original SER buildings are still standing on the western side (top). This was the site of the only platform when it opened, with the opposite platform added a few years later. The buildings on the eastern side were built around 1911 by the South Eastern & Chatham Railway, following the merger of the SER and the London, Chatham & Dover Railway in 1899. The new building featured an imposing clock tower, seen here under maintenance, which dwarfed the rest of the station. This building contains passenger facilities, whilst the original houses the current ticket office.

From 1923 the suffix "Central" was added to its name to distinguish it from the other station in the town, also then known as Tunbridge Wells. This was built by the SER's rival, the London, Brighton & South Coast Railway, in 1866. It became "Tunbridge Wells West" in 1923 when the LB&SCR and the SE&CR became part of the Southern Railway. This was a much larger station, with 5 platforms. The station building (bottom image, inset) had a large 3-storey clock tower on the eastern side. The two were connected by a single line track through the 287 yard Grove Tunnel in 1876.

Tunbridge Wells West was to close on July 6th 1985, but part of the line has been restored as the Spa Valley Railway heritage line, opened in December 1996. The station now has a small new platform, paid for by the adjacent supermarket which was built on the old goods yard. It operates out of the listed 1891 four-track engine shed, which is visible in the top right of the picture. The listed station building is still standing to the east of the site, but is now a pub cum restaurant.

Tunbridge Wells:

Opened: 25/11/1846

Platforms: 2

Passengers (Ranking):
2008/9: 3,795,156 (85)
2007/8: 3,809,211 (79)
2006/7: 3,450,304 (83)
2005/6: 3,264,797 (76)
2004/5: 3,149,435 (78)

Wakefield Kirkgate

Opened: 05/10/1840

Platforms: 3

Passengers (Ranking):
2008/9: 465,978 (767)
2007/8: 360,356 (843)
2006/7:   769 (2461)
2005/6:   564 (2454)
2004/5:   372 (2457)

Wakefield Westgate Figures:
2008/9: 2,017,854 (205)
2007/8: 1,610,947 (257)
2006/7: 1,877,981 (205)
2005/6: 1,846,988 (160)
2004/5: 1,760,373 (167)

rkgate station has definitely seen better days. Although the ticket fice and station buildings are Grade II listed, the rest of the station is a large state of disrepair. The station was built by the Manchester & eds Railway in 1840, but after they were absorbed by the Lancashire Yorkshire Railway in July 1847 the station would end up being jointly n. The L&YR & the Great Northern Railway became responsible for rkgate on August 23rd 1853 and promptly set about rebuilding the ation. The main station buildings (lower left centre) were rebuilt in a assical style with a sandstone façade, and the platforms were rebuilt include three faces, including an island platform on the south side ight). The platforms and the two central through lines were all covered a large iron roof. This was demolished in 1972, but the supporting all on the island platform remains in place. Also visible in this picture the old engine shed on the northern side (upper left centre),

consisting of the smaller, two-pitched roof building and the long single pitched roof structure, both located behind platform 1. This was demolished in 2008 to make way for a new Network Rail depot. The station today is unstaffed, and possibly unloved. It has been overtaken by Wakefield Westgate as the city's main rail hub. Westgate opened in 1867 on the opposite side of town, and despite being smaller, having only two platforms, it has the majority of the services. The passenger figures for Kirkgate station in the information box are correct. Between 2004 and 2007 tickets in Wakefield were sold as "Wakefield Stations", meaning either Kirkgate or Westgate. As Kirkgate was unstaffed no tickets would have been directly sold there, so the true figures for usage are not known, and thus register as less than 1,000. Since 2007 more accurate ways of calculating the totals have been introduced. The figures for tickets at Westgate have been included for reference.

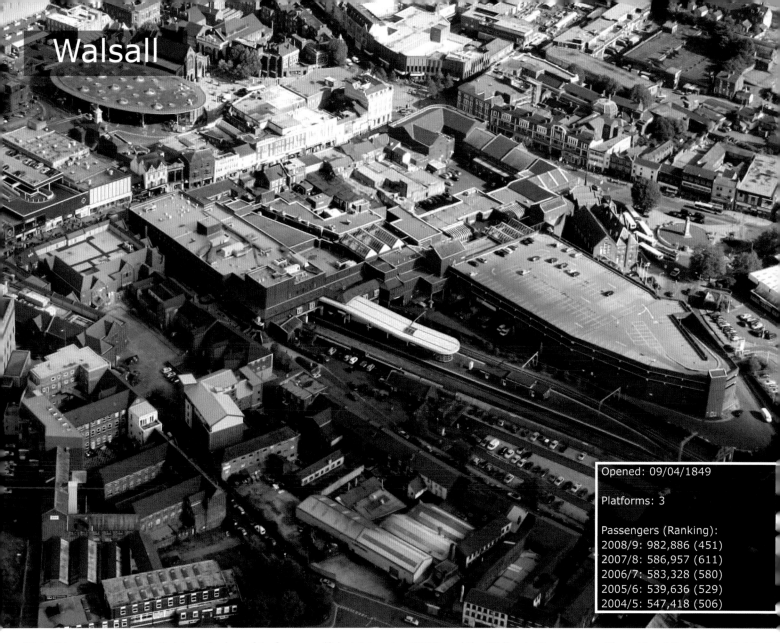

Walsall

Opened: 09/04/1849

Platforms: 3

Passengers (Ranking):
2008/9: 982,886 (451)
2007/8: 586,957 (611)
2006/7: 583,328 (580)
2005/6: 539,636 (529)
2004/5: 547,418 (506)

Walsall is another station that is a shadow of its former self, but it is not as bad as it was shortly after the large shopping centre that now sits over it was built. When this centre was built, from 1978-1980, Walsall was reduced to being barely a couple of concrete platforms where once there had been a proud and elegant station. Around this time there were very little services to the station left. Many lines had closed in the area under Beeching and the future looked bleak. Services began to increase again during the 1980s, and the station is now at least comfortable. In 1995 rebuilding works saw the creation of an interesting curved, glazed waiting room on the remaining island platform, underneath a new white canopy. There was also a new booking hall and other passenger facilities that could be accessed directly from the shopping centre. In its heyday the station had a total of 7 platforms (5 through and two bay), as well as central through lines for freight and associated goods yards for the

LNWR and the Midland. These were either side of the tracks slightly to the south, but none of them survive today. The town was initially bypassed when the railways came to the area. The first was built by the Grand Junction Railway in 1837, but it did not come into the town centre and the nearest station was at Bescott Bridge (now near Wednesbury, slightly to the south west of Walsall). It wasn't until the South Staffordshire Railway opened in 1847 that Walsall was finally connected to the rail network. The SSR would later become part of the LNWR, and they widened the station to allow fast moving freight lines to be built in the centre in the early 1860s. The Midland began to use the station around 1872, and in conjunction with the LNWR the main station buildings were rebuilt in 1883 in an Elizabethan style. All of this history was lost, however, when the programme of "improvements" was completed in 1980.

Whitley Bay

Opened: 03/07/1882

Closed: 10/09/1979

Reopened: 11/08/1980

Platforms: 2

This impressive little station is no longer on the national rail network and is instead part of the Tyne & Wear Metro system. It was opened by the North Eastern Railway in 1882, replacing an earlier station built by the Blyth & Tyne Railway near Hillheads Road around 1862 (The B&TR was absorbed by the NER in 1874). The original station was smaller in area than the current layout, but still only had two platforms. It opened as "Whitley" and did not adopt the name "Whitley Bay" until July 1st 1899, around a year after the town changed its name to avoid being confused with Whitby further down the coast. The present structures date from 1910 when the station was rebuilt by the NER to architect William Bell's design. Opened on October 9th of that year, the impressive main building, with its elegant façade and Baroque central clock tower, are now Grade II listed, as is the glazed roof over the platforms. It remained in operation on the rail network until closing in September 1979 for conversion to the new Metro system. The station remains relatively unaltered inside, with its spacious platforms bathed in light from the ornate roof. One difference is the presence of a triptych mosaic on the bays of the former booking hall ticket windows that now add a dash of colour to the interior. Whitley Bay station is on the Yellow Route of the Metro System, on a route that loops from Newcastle City Centre to North Shields, via Whitley Bay, back through Newcastle and then south to South Shields. It reopened for service on August 11th 1980 and continues to be an important stop on the system.

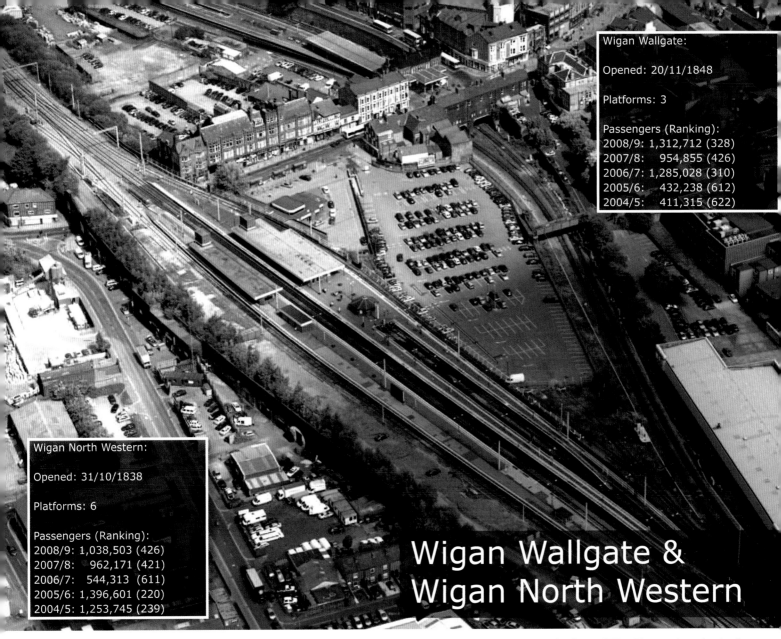

Wigan Wallgate:

Opened: 20/11/1848

Platforms: 3

Passengers (Ranking):
2008/9: 1,312,712 (328)
2007/8:   954,855 (426)
2006/7: 1,285,028 (310)
2005/6:   432,238 (612)
2004/5:   411,315 (622)

Wigan North Western:

Opened: 31/10/1838

Platforms: 6

Passengers (Ranking):
2008/9: 1,038,503 (426)
2007/8:   962,171 (421)
2006/7:   544,313 (611)
2005/6: 1,396,601 (220)
2004/5: 1,253,745 (239)

Wigan Wallgate & Wigan North Western

Wigan's two remaining stations sit almost side by side on the edge of the town centre. With the lines merging just to the east (bottom right) it begs the question why they couldn't have been built side-by side and formed one larger station? North Western station was the first to be built, and opened in 1838 by the North Union Railway, an amalgamation of the Wigan Branch Railway and the Wigan & Preston Junction Railway, the first in the UK. Wallgate station was opened by the Lancashire & Yorkshire ten years later, but was originally located around 100 yards further west next to Dorning Street (off image, towards top left). The land next to North Western, now a car park, was already home to a goods yard and sidings, leaving little room at the time Wallgate was built. It was rebuilt on its present site in 1896, opening on February 2nd, with the entrance building and its glazed porte-cochere at street level on Wallgate. The old platform buildings and roof were removed

following modernisation in the late 1970s. The station also had an additional short platform used mostly for stabling on the south side. Th is now filled in and used as a car park (top left). North Western curren has 6 platforms, but at its largest had 10 (5 through and 5 bay). The southern-most platform (bottom) was much wider than it is now, and footprint can still be seen to the left where there is a newer through line. This platform had two bays on the east and one on the west, and there was an additional facing platform to the south. The station was also covered by a large roof with latticework iron girders, but sadly thi was removed following a rebuild in 1972. Wigan did have a third large station on the northern side of the town centre. It was known as Wiga Central (03/10/1892 – 02/11/1964) and was built by the Manchester, Sheffield & Lincolnshire Railway.

The wealthy commuter town of Wilmslow is a regular stop on the West Coast Main Line, although not all WCML services call here. The station was built as a part of the Manchester & Birmingham Railway and opened in 1842. Initially there were only two platforms which were later connected by a footbridge on the south side. The railway crossed the valley of the River Bollin to the north by means of an 11-arch viaduct constructed by George Watson Buck (lower right centre, main image). Like his much larger viaduct just to the north in Stockport, the viaduct was built of red brick with stone dressings. It is know a Grade II listed structure. The land now occupied by the car park on the western side was originally a coal depot used for storing deposits brought from the nearby colliery at Poynton, just to the north east. There was also a railway hotel, which has since been demolished with the land being redeveloped as modern offices (top centre, by the main road). The station was extended westwards to 4 platforms with the opening of the Styal Loop Line in 1909. This was built to relieve congestion on the overcrowded Stockport to Manchester routes, which were hampered by there being only 4 tracks on the Stockport Viaduct. This resulted in the closure of the coal depot at Wilmslow, as there was no longer enough room once the works had been completed. The Styal Line necessitated the building of a second viaduct in almost identical style on the western side. This new viaduct was built in blue engineering brick, and can be seen sitting parallel with the original on the right of the image. Today the footbridge has gone, and all platforms are now accessed by a subway.

Opened: 10/05/1842

Platforms: 4

Passengers (Ranking):
2008/9: 750,434 (564)
2007/8: 685,684 (541)
2006/7: 499,394 (635)
2005/6: 532,652 (532)
2004/5: 569,820 (496)

Wilmslow

Wolverhampton

Opened: 24/06/1852

Platforms: 6

Passengers (Ranking):
2008/9: 4,221,010 (73)
2007/8: 2,510,429 (148)
2006/7: 2,399,955 (143)
2005/6: 2,254,742 (117)
2004/5: 2,058,706 (125)

Wolverhampton station was opened by the Shrewsbury & Birmingham Railway in 1852 and was the first major station in the city. A second would be opened just two years later on a piece of adjacent land slightly to the north east. This became known as "Wolverhampton Low Level" station, whilst the first became known as "Wolverhampton High Level". The Low Level station was constructed jointly by the Birmingham, Worcester & Dudley Railway, the Oxford, Worcester & Wolverhampton Railway, and the Shrewsbury & Birmingham Railway, and originally featured both standard and broad gauge tracks – the most northerly of all of the broad gauges. The station building was in an impressive Italianate style made out of blue engineering brick. This building still stands (top right) and is Grade II listed. The Low Level station closed on March 6th 1972, although it remained open until 1981 as a parcel depot. The land to the rear has now been redeveloped into a mixed office and residential development as part of the Canalside Quarter. High Level was completely rebuilt in the mid 1960s, which included demolition of the old overall roof in February 1965 along with the original façade. Since the closure of the Low Level station it has been known simply as "Wolverhampton". In 2004 a further facing platform was built on the north eastern side along with a new footbridge to all platforms (left). Just to the west of the site is the old Oxley Depot (right). Opened in 1907, it is now used for maintaining carriages for Virgin Trains on their West Coast Main Line routes.

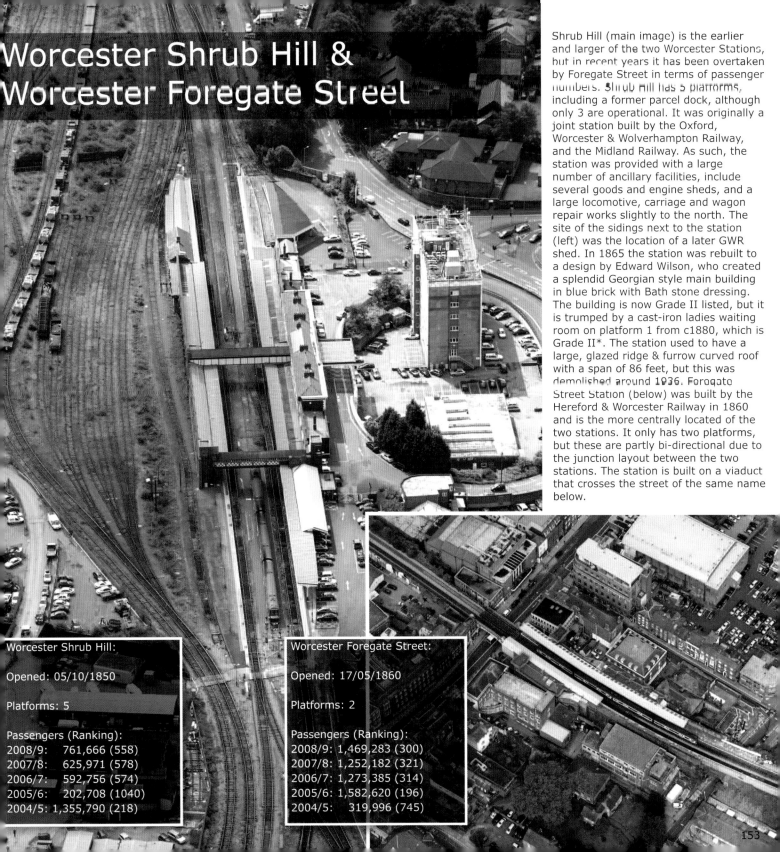

Worcester Shrub Hill & Worcester Foregate Street

Shrub Hill (main image) is the earlier and larger of the two Worcester Stations, but in recent years it has been overtaken by Foregate Street in terms of passenger numbers. Shrub Hill has 5 platforms, including a former parcel dock, although only 3 are operational. It was originally a joint station built by the Oxford, Worcester & Wolverhampton Railway, and the Midland Railway. As such, the station was provided with a large number of ancillary facilities, include several goods and engine sheds, and a large locomotive, carriage and wagon repair works slightly to the north. The site of the sidings next to the station (left) was the location of a later GWR shed. In 1865 the station was rebuilt to a design by Edward Wilson, who created a splendid Georgian style main building in blue brick with Bath stone dressing. The building is now Grade II listed, but it is trumped by a cast-iron ladies waiting room on platform 1 from c1880, which is Grade II*. The station used to have a large, glazed ridge & furrow curved roof with a span of 86 feet, but this was demolished around 1936. Foregate Street Station (below) was built by the Hereford & Worcester Railway in 1860 and is the more centrally located of the two stations. It only has two platforms, but these are partly bi-directional due to the junction layout between the two stations. The station is built on a viaduct that crosses the street of the same name below.

Worcester Shrub Hill:

Opened: 05/10/1850

Platforms: 5

Passengers (Ranking):
2008/9:   761,666 (558)
2007/8:   625,971 (578)
2006/7:   592,756 (574)
2005/6:   202,708 (1040)
2004/5: 1,355,790 (218)

Worcester Foregate Street:

Opened: 17/05/1860

Platforms: 2

Passengers (Ranking):
2008/9: 1,469,283 (300)
2007/8: 1,252,182 (321)
2006/7: 1,273,385 (314)
2005/6: 1,582,620 (196)
2004/5:   319,996 (745)

York is one of the most important railway cities in Great Britain and it has one of its most magnificent stations. Covering a vast area, the station is just a small part of a once huge complex that was devoted to the production, maintenance and utilisation of the railways. The station's most impressive feature is its enormous multi span iron and glass roof, similar in style to that found at Newcastle Central. The size of the roof shows the scope of the original platforms that were built in 1877 when the station opened. They were considerably smaller than they are now, but were later extended at both ends, with the longest now almost double its original length. There are currently 11 platforms, but at its largest the station had 17. In the late 1980s a number of bay platforms on the north eastern side of the station were removed (top right, under the smallest roof span), and the rest of the platforms inside the shed were remodelled. Built by the North Eastern Railway, the station was a collaboration between the architects Thomas Prosser and William Peachey. The main entrance (far right) contains a nine-arch porte-cochere and is built from yellow Scarborough brick. It is quite a modest entrance when compared to other grand stations, but as the station was the largest in the world upon completion it did not necessarily require a "statement building" at the front, particularly when it had such an impressive interior. Peachey and Prosser were also responsible for the Royal York Hotel (right middle) in 1878, which is built in the same Scarborough brick as the station. The hotel was extended in 1896 when a new wing was added on the north western side. It is now Grade II listed, whilst York Station is Grade II* listed. The footbridge in the centre of the station was added in 1938 and links directly to the National Railway Museum at the top of the photo.

Opened: 25/06/1877

Platforms: 11

Passengers (Ranking):
2008/9: 6,802,004 (41)
2007/8: 6,534,388 (42)
2006/7: 6,363,387 (41)
2005/6: 6,148,333 (34)
2004/5: 5,795,978 (37)

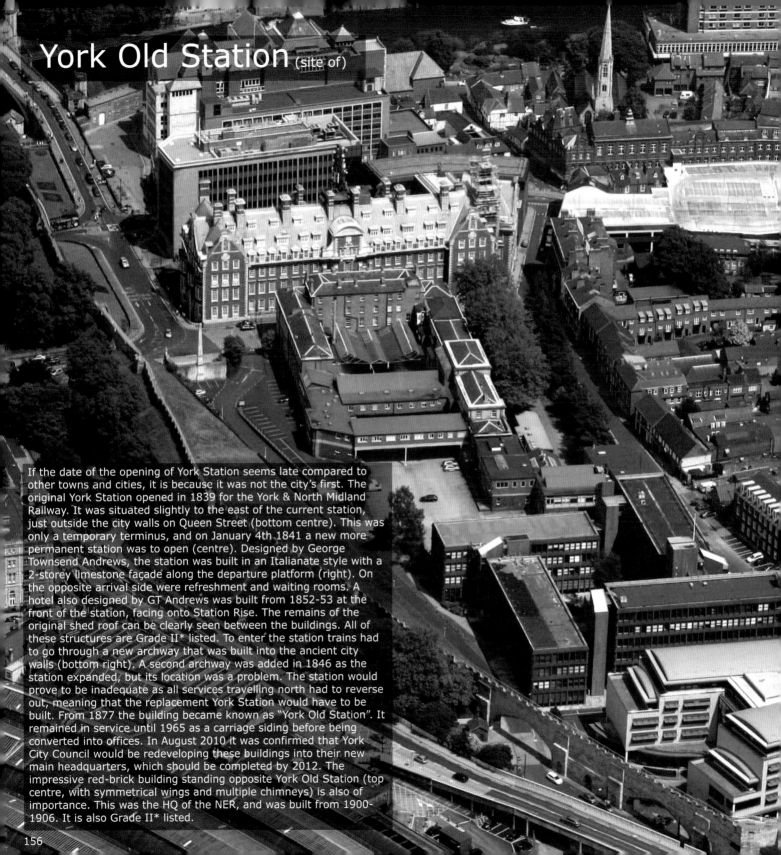

York Old Station (site of)

If the date of the opening of York Station seems late compared to other towns and cities, it is because it was not the city's first. The original York Station opened in 1839 for the York & North Midland Railway. It was situated slightly to the east of the current station, just outside the city walls on Queen Street (bottom centre). This was only a temporary terminus, and on January 4th 1841 a new more permanent station was to open (centre). Designed by George Townsend Andrews, the station was built in an Italianate style with a 2-storey limestone façade along the departure platform (right). On the opposite arrival side were refreshment and waiting rooms. A hotel also designed by GT Andrews was built from 1852-53 at the front of the station, facing onto Station Rise. The remains of the original shed roof can be clearly seen between the buildings. All of these structures are Grade II* listed. To enter the station trains had to go through a new archway that was built into the ancient city walls (bottom right). A second archway was added in 1846 as the station expanded, but its location was a problem. The station would prove to be inadequate as all services travelling north had to reverse out, meaning that the replacement York Station would have to be built. From 1877 the building became known as "York Old Station". It remained in service until 1965 as a carriage siding before being converted into offices. In August 2010 it was confirmed that York City Council would be redeveloping these buildings into their new main headquarters, which should be completed by 2012. The impressive red-brick building standing opposite York Old Station (top centre, with symmetrical wings and multiple chimneys) is also of importance. This was the HQ of the NER, and was built from 1900-1906. It is also Grade II* listed.

National Railway Museum - York

tuated immediately to the west of York Station is the site of the rmer York North Traction Maintenance Depot. It was also known as rk Leeman Road Depot. The road was named after George Leeman, ho was Chairman of the NER when York station was built, as well as a rmer MP for York. The depot was opened in 1878 by the North astern Railway and would go on to be their major manufacturing ntre. At its largest the site included a vast engine shed to the north Jo 3 shed), an equally vast goods shed in the middle (No 4 shed), two rge wagon works amidst mile after mile of sidings on the western de, and a truly gigantic carriage works on the south east of the site, hich was almost as big as all of the other sheds put together. This ew, looking north east, shows the engine shed (left, with the white of) and the goods shed (centre), along with one of the former wagon

works sheds (bottom middle). The carriage shed was just off image, in the bottom right. Much of the depot is now home to the National Railway Museum, which opened in 1975. The museum is based mainly in the old Nos 3 & 4 sheds in the north of the site, along with a series of other smaller buildings, and covers an area of around 20 acres, a fraction of the original depot. There has been a railway museum on the site since 1928, which housed archive materials and rolling stock from the NER's own collections. It was situated in a former erecting and repair shed on the eastern side of the main line tracks into York Station, just off the bottom right. In 1975 this was combined with the collection housed in the old British Rail "Museum of British Transport" in Clapham, London, to make up the new national museum.

National Railway Museum - York

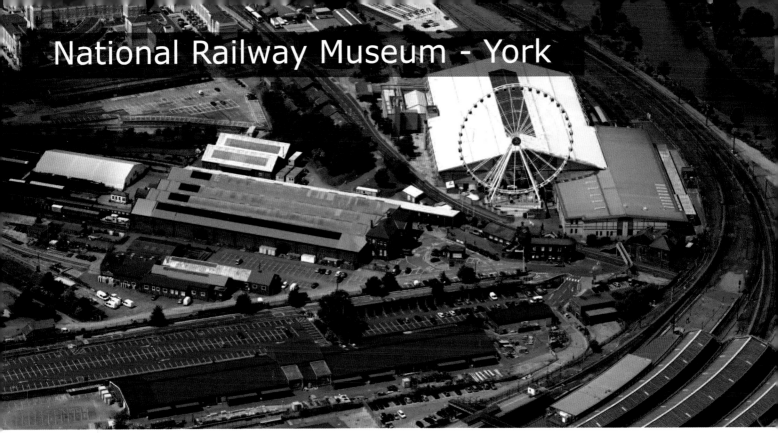

This image shows a closer view of the main museum site. The engine shed (right centre) is now known as "The Great Hall", where the majority of the museum's locomotives are stored. There is also one of the remaining turntables, which was added in 1954. The building was rebuilt during the 1950s, but by 1990 its roof was beginning to weaken and so had to be replaced. Whilst work on the new roof was underway the old goods shed (centre), which had previously been used for storage, was opened for public display for the first time. When the roof was completed in 1992 it was decided to keep the goods shed open, and it was renamed to "The Station Hall". This building features many interesting items of rolling stock as if they were sitting in a station, including various Royal trains and carriages including those used by Queen Victoria and Queen Elizabeth II. In total there are over 100 locos and another 200 pieces of rolling stock at York. Many of the locomotives are still rail worthy and can be rolled out for special occasions, either here or elsewhere in the country. Most of the rolling stock is based in the York arm of the museum, but different items are often displayed at the Shildon branch. The world famous Mallard is currently on display at Shildon. On the far right, adjoining The Great Hall, is the combined "Warehouse" and workshop building, which is known as "The Works". The Warehouse section (on the right) is another area displaying locomotives, as well as other items of railway paraphernalia. The Works (on the left of this building) is the museum's maintenance and engineering building, which is open to the public. At the time of writing, the iconic Flying Scotsman is currently being restored here. The museum also has an extensive library housing over 20,000 railway related books, as well as an important archive section, where original drawings and plans from railway companies and manufacturers are kept. These include blueprints of engines, stations and railway buildings and structures.

Purchasing Images

All of the images in this book are available for purchase, either prints or for reproduction.

Please visit **www.webbaviation.co.uk** to browse for images and use the online shopping cart, or send an email quoting reference "SFTA" and the page number of the image in the book to

sales@webbaviation.co.uk

ISBN: 978-0-9557265-2